ELICITING
EXCELLENCE

Bringing Out the Best in People

MICHAEL J. BECK

Eliciting Excellence.

© Michael J. Beck 2015

ISBN: 978-1-68222-967-5 Print

ISBN: 978-1-68222-968-2 eBook

Printed in the United States of America

www.elicitingexcellence.com

TABLE OF CONTENTS

INTRODUCTION

Like most people, I began my first job bright-eyed, enthusiastic, and ready to make a difference. I worked hard and tried to be as diligent and creative as I could. But I had a boss who didn't seem to appreciate my work or the insights I had. He wore his long hours at work as a badge of sacrifice and a sign of loyalty. (On a side note, a few years after I left the company, he died of a heart attack at a young age.) He was resentful of the success others had and had no problem making his feelings known. Consequently, I soon became disillusioned, ambivalent, and disheartened.

*A couple of years into my job, I had had enough and left the company. I thought that perhaps joining a smaller company would be a good way to avoid poor leadership, so I went to work for one. Was I ever wrong! But not in the way you might expect. You see, I discovered that **I** was a poor leader!*

In fact, I was a terrible leader. I really hadn't been around any good leaders to emulate. I could only model the poor leadership I had seen up until then. I was a poor communicator, an uncaring leader focused on self over others, and someone who really didn't have a clue about interpersonal effectiveness. Worst of all, I wasn't even aware I was poor at leading, communicating, or caring. I was clueless.

As I gained more experience, I came to have an appreciation for just how poor a leader I was, and my leadership shortcomings really began to bother me. I saw that my leadership style didn't reflect who I was as a person, and I made a conscious decision to improve myself and my effectiveness.

Over the ensuing years, I strove to improve my communication effectiveness. I became more empathetic towards the people I worked with, I learned how to read people, I learned how to develop people, and I began to think more strategically.

I made the shift from a poor leader to an admired leader in several ways. I read books on leadership, communication, and interpersonal effectiveness. I made note when a leader did something or said something that had a positive effect on me or others and made note when their actions and words had a negative effect. I practiced the behaviors I admired, even though sometimes it took me out of my comfort zone. And I owned up to my mistakes, apologizing to people when I didn't do what I knew I should have done. This transformation took many years—decades, in fact. I didn't have the advantages of assessments, coaches, or mentors. But the effort to transform has been well worth the effort.

Over the years since my transformation, I've given a lot of thought to leadership and the difference that good leadership makes in the success of a business and in people's lives. Although much has been written about leadership and how important good leadership is, it occurred to me that nowhere had I ever read *why* good leadership matters. After a good deal of reflection, I came to understand why and how leadership makes a difference, and I've reduced this insight down to one simple statement:

Exceptional leadership elicits excellence.

Great leaders bring out the best in people. Great leaders help people be their best by who they are, how they interact with people, and how they guide the organization. An organization led by highly effective leaders is highly engaged, highly creative, highly productive, and highly profitable.

I'm passionate about helping people become better leaders. I'm passionate about helping people reach their full potential. I'm passionate about helping leaders help others realize their potential. And I'm passionate about helping people treat others better. It's my way of making a difference in the world, and I'm hoping it's your way of making a difference as well.

This book lays the foundation for any leader to become more effective. We'll cover the many ways of bringing out the best in people, we'll cover how to become better at those competencies, and we'll cover how and where to start. If you apply these principles for bringing out the best in people (and becoming your best in the process), you will have more success, less stress, greater satisfaction, and more enjoyment in business and in life. My hope is that you will put these insights into action and make a real difference to people.

- Michael J. Beck
Portland, Oregon
November, 2015
mbeck@michaeljbeck.com
www.michaeljbeck.com

CHAPTER 1: THE BOTTOM LINE

Why bringing out the best in people matters

The idea that bringing out the best in people is a good thing is a concept that no one would really argue with. The challenge is that unless we really understand the importance of it, the values and behaviors that accomplish it often get put on the back burner while more pressing financial matters take our attention and focus. But there are some very compelling reasons which ought to keep the efforts to bring out the best in people at the forefront at all times. The reasons have to do with the effective execution of strategic plans. The better people perform, the greater the results an organization will achieve.

Susan was frustrated. Revenues and profits had stalled after a promising start to her initiative. It was especially perplexing, since she had given things quite a bit of thought and worked hard to get strong "buy-in" throughout the company.

She had spent good deal of time working to understand the core issues her organization faced and then tapped into the collective brainpower of the company to develop meaningful strategies to address each issue. Once the strategic direction was decided upon, the needed courses of action were identified, financial viability was ascertained, and the required resources were secured.

And then, with great fanfare and excitement, the plan was rolled out to the organization. Goals and accountability were established, and the wheels of progress were put into motion. At first, everything and everyone seemed to be working well. People were taking action. Progress meetings were held. And results began to improve.

But then something happened. Progress began to peter out. Although it seemed the plan was still on track, growth began to stall. And why it stalled seemed a mystery.

The issue may have been one of complacency after the initial enthusiasm had faded. Or maybe "turf wars" had broken out, with people pursuing their own interests. It could be that the organization as a whole lacked the same sense of focus and urgency embraced by the C-Suite. Or it may have been a prevailing reluctance within the workforce to make the necessary changes required for success. Any one of these issues may have been at play.

On top of all the potential internal issues is the likelihood that the landscape of the market may have shifted. Technology continued to evolve. New competitors came upon the scene. And economic conditions were ever-changing. Each of these conditions presented unforeseen obstacles, and overcoming these obstacles required flexibility, adaptability, and creativity. The bottom line for Susan was that results weren't what they should have been.

Scenarios similar to the one above play out fairly regularly throughout the corporate world. And as every executive knows, wanting better results and actually achieving them can be very different things.

Some executives find developing a great strategy easier than creating a plan of execution, and others find the plan easier to develop, but pretty much every executive acknowledges that effectively executing a strategic plan is the most challenging effort.

The results gained from executing a sound strategy (assuming all the needed resources are in place), are dependent upon four critical factors: speed of implementation, consistency of effort, quality of performance, and flexibility.

Speed of Implementation

Speed of implementation is especially important if there is a low barrier to entry. In other words, if competition can easily enter the market with a comparable solution, then being first to market gives an organization a decided advantage.

In order to accomplish this, there must be a sense of urgency in executing a plan. Executing swiftly requires the organization to be (and remain) engaged, focused, and productive. Without this focus, the other day-to-day activities tend to distract a team from working on those things that bring the organization closer to achieving its strategic objectives.

Consistency of Effort

Consistency of effort is essential for achieving strong results because rarely will ambitious goals be achieved in a short period of time. Sustained effort—or more accurately, sustained purposeful effort— is needed over a longer length of time.

It's analogous to the task of rolling a heavy ball up a hill. As soon as the effort stops, the ball rolls back to the bottom, all the progress already achieved is lost, and the effort begins all over again, requiring extra effort to overcome inertia and once again make progress.

Additionally, it is often necessary for a tipping point to be reached in order for a new concept or product to be widely accepted. Efforts must remain consistent while this tipping point is slowly advanced upon. This persistence of effort is dependent once again upon the workforce remaining engaged and resilient. A purpose-driven organization is required for effort to remain consistent—especially when progress is not apparent or self-evident.

Quality of Performance

Quality of performance is essential in the execution of a strategic initiative. It relates to the nature of the solutions developed to overcome the inevitable obstacles, setbacks, and disappointments that arise while executing a strategy. And the quality of the solutions developed in response to these challenges determines the level of results gained.

Creativity and positivity are essential for uncovering the best solutions. Creative thinking spawns solutions that go beyond incremental improvement and can lead to order-of-magnitude increases. Additionally, a positive attitude tends to keep people focused on solutions. A negative attitude conversely tends to keep people focused on the obstacles.

Developing effective solutions depends on the ability to differentiate between symptoms and problems. It requires clarity of thought and the determination to keep digging until the core issues causing the obstacles are uncovered. The only way to have people be creative, positive, persistent, and clear-headed is to bring out their best. It results in high engagement.

Flexibility

Flexibility is necessary for success because the business landscape is always changing. Course corrections are required as the economy shifts, new technologies emerge, new competitors appear, and customer preferences evolve.

The successful modification of plans depends on an openness to and an acceptance of change. If people are mired in mediocrity, moving out of the comfort of routine becomes nearly impossible. When people are performing at their best—both in thought and action—change is taken in stride.

People who simply do the required work and are ambivalent about initiatives tend to produce acceptable results, while those who are passionate about what they do—spending their discretionary time and effort looking for solutions and efficiencies—tend to produce outstanding results. The distinction is evident when we reflect on our own efforts and results. At times, when we are just fulfilling our obligations, the results are generally just satisfactory, and our efforts drain our energies and emotions. In contrast, when we are completely engaged with a project or task, we lose track of time, can't stop thinking about it, are energized by the effort, and achieve notable results. Bringing out the best in people matters.

If we reflect on the behaviors that ensure speed, consistency, quality, and flexibility, they include things like collaboration, adaptability, creativity, communication, dedication, pride, and productivity. Engagement fosters most of these behaviors, and the many positive behaviors that engagement brings with it are essential to getting stronger results from the execution of a strategy.

However, the mere presence of these behaviors doesn't guarantee great results. The reality is that their impact on success is directly related to the *strength* of these behaviors, which is directly related to how engaged the people are within an organization and whether they are putting forth their best effort.

The bottom line is that if you want to maximize results, you must maximize engagement by bringing out the best in people and getting them to put forth their best effort.

The concept of engagement and bringing out the best in people is not a "feel good" issue. It is a strategic issue that drives the bottom line. A recent study on employee engagement conducted by the Gallup organization reported that the ROI of companies with high engagement was *2.5 times* that of companies with poor engagement!

Consider this remarkable example of Campbell Soup's experience with engagement:

In 2001, Campbell Soup Company was a stodgy, slow-growth company. They discovered that for every engaged employee, they had three who were ambivalent or disengaged. Over the course of the next eight years, they reversed their level of engagement to a point where they had 23 engaged employees for each one who was disengaged. How did that translate into financial results? Over those eight years, the S&P 500 dropped 10%, while Campbell Soup's stock rose 30%.

In the chapters that follow, we'll examine how to avoid disengagement and how to bring out the best in people.

CHAPTER 2: AVOIDING DISENGAGEMENT

The causes of disillusionment and disengagement

The meeting started the same way most of the department meetings started. Sarah and four of her co-workers arrived five minutes before the hour. As usual, Fred was late to his own meeting. Although they all expected it, they were all annoyed. After all, everyone was busy with projects and deadlines. The meetings often seemed fairly pointless, so making everyone wait made it even more frustrating. Fred strolled in at 10:07, coffee in hand and talking on the phone. Sarah and the others sat in silence while Fred finished the call, which seemed to be about getting together for lunch with a buddy.

"OK, let's get started," Fred announced, not even bothering to apologize for being late. No one was quite sure of the purpose of the meeting, so they waited to hear the agenda. "I need an update from everyone about the progress on the new product line. Jim (head of the engineering team), have you and Tom (head of the manufacturing team) worked out your differences?" Jim and Tom glanced at one another. Jim spoke first, "No, not really. We've made some progress but haven't been able to reach a compromise on the component details." Fred rolled his eyes and began chastising them both. "You know, you guys are like

a couple of children who want their own way. Why can't two grown men reach an agreement on something as straightforward as this? It makes me question whether I have the right people heading up your teams. Either get this straightened out or you'll both be looking for new jobs!" The two men stared at the table, feeling embarrassed and demeaned.

"Sarah, what about finance? Have you finished the financial forecast for this rollout?" "Fred," Sarah replied, "didn't you get the email I sent this morning? I stayed up half the night getting it to you so you'd have time to review it." "I did see it come in," Fred apologized, "but just thought it would be easier to hear it directly from you." Sarah struggled to hide her frustration and began summarizing the results of her forecast. About halfway through, Fred interrupted. "Sarah, I'm just not following this, and we really don't have time for all the details right now. I guess I'll have to read through what you sent and get back to you."

"Karen, where do things stand with the marketing strategy?" "Well, Jim," Karen began, "as you know, the key to grabbing a strong market share is to clearly differentiate this product from the others in the marketplace. It hasn't been as easy as we had hoped. For one thing, we're not completely clear yet on all the unique points available for us to really grab onto. The team's been a bit frustrated. One thought we had is to—" Fred interrupted, "Karen, let me tell you what we need to do. My thoughts are to position it as a whole new product. A '2.0' kind of thing. I'd like you and your team to start working on that angle. When do you think you can have something for me to review?" Feeling cornered, Karen committed to a two-week time frame.

"Great!" Fred exclaimed. I know we can deliver this project on time and under budget. I believe in all of you! Go out there and make it happen!" And with that, Fred got up, turned and walked out the door. Barbara, head of IT, had been sitting quietly taking everything in. Not only had Fred not called on her, but since her department wasn't directly involved in the new project, she wasn't even sure why she had been asked to attend. Now that the meeting had adjourned, she felt it truly had been a waste of time for her. She got up, clearly displeased, and returned to her office, leaving the other four sitting in silence.

Sarah was the first to speak. "Karen, I can't believe he didn't even let you explain what you and your team came up with. What a jerk!" "Yeah, I know. It was pretty dismissive of him," Karen replied. "Dismissive? I thought he was a total ass to you, Karen. If he wanted to dictate the direction to you, why did he waste your team's time trying to come up with something original?"

"At least he didn't belittle you in front of everyone like he did with me and Jim," Tom chimed in. "I know none of us wants to lose his job, but Fred really makes it hard to come into work every day with a positive attitude. He just doesn't understand the competing interests Jim and I are trying to iron out. We've tried to get him involved to get his perspective and priorities, but he never has time for us." Jim piped up, "We're trying to do the right thing and what's best for the company, but Fred's only out for Fred. It's hard to respect someone who takes all the credit and points fingers when things go wrong."

Coming to Fred's defense, Sarah spoke up, "Well, I think Fred is just really busy and can't get to everything he'd like to." It was too much for Karen to take in silence. "Sarah! Let me get this straight. This is the most important initiative of the year, you worked half the night to get him all the information he needed, and he was 'too busy' to look it over?! That's B.S.! Frankly, I don't trust or respect that guy. I can't figure out how he got the promotion to begin with."

They all nodded in agreement and sat for a moment. Then Sarah and the others stood, feeling frustrated and a bit disillusioned, and returned to their respective offices, resigned to continue the work they'd been tasked to do by Fred.

Although the events in the story above are a stereotype, no doubt we've all worked for bosses who acted in a manner similar to what transpired. We've all heard the expression, "People don't quit companies, they quit bosses," and it generally holds true. The reason is that most people begin working at a company with high expectations and high aspirations but become disillusioned with their boss. The boss—the person who employees interact with most—sets the tone for their work environment and either brings out the best in people or stifles their engagement.

This dynamic rarely has anything to do with a leader's intelligence, education, knowledge, or experience. Instead, it has to do with the leader's character and how the leader interacts with those around him or her. A leader's level of interpersonal competence generally determines their effectiveness as a leader. A leader who has a strong, positive character earns people's trust and respect. A leader who excels at interpersonal skills will more easily keep people engaged, productive, and loyal.

Avoiding Disengagement

Consider this: if we've done a good job selecting new hires, then they're excited to be there, enthused about the work they'll be doing, and they're fantasizing about how they'll make a difference in the company. In short, they're highly engaged when they start.

Therefore, if people are highly engaged at the start, our job as leaders is to keep from screwing things up. In other words, our job as a leader is to keep people from becoming disengaged.

Why does disengagement occur? Disengagement generally occurs for one of two reasons (or both). Either someone's boss does or says (or doesn't do or say) something that causes a person to become less engaged or someone's company does (or doesn't do) something that causes them to be less engaged. The actions and behaviors which either enhance or diminish engagement correspond to Maslow's Hierarchy of Needs—both in classification and in importance. Maslow classified these needs into five categories: physiological, security, belonging, self-esteem, and self-fulfillment. His premise was that that these needs are universal. Additionally, he argued, the more basic needs of a person must be addressed before the other needs matter. To put it in perspective, being appreciated won't matter much if a person fears their financial stability and security are in jeopardy.

Physiological

From an organizational perspective, physiological needs are addressed with compensation and benefits. Offering compensation, which allows a person to provide food and shelter for themselves and their family, along with providing benefits, which address a person's health needs, both go towards meeting an individual's physiological needs.

Security

Several factors impact whether a person's security needs are met. Although employee safety is a factor, relatively few workplace situations or environments would be cause for concerns about physical safety. When it is an issue, it will need to be addressed before any other need will matter.

More common is the issue of job security. Employment security relates to a person's feeling of how likely the company is to succeed, along with their feeling about how secure their position is in the eyes of the company and their boss.

If a company's future is uncertain, people's attentions are often turned towards finding a new opportunity. This concern is often coupled with a concern about losing the income to meet their physiological needs. Likewise, if employees fear retribution for speaking up and feel neither the company nor their boss cares about them, their need for job security is unfulfilled.

Belonging

Belonging needs are reflected in the need to be accepted and to be part of something. People feel they belong when they're involved in activities and decisions. When an individual is ostracized, engagement diminishes. When people aren't included in the decision-making process, they feel unimportant and undervalued.

The need to belong is also fulfilled when people feel accepted. And people feel accepted when they feel respected and trusted. If someone feels they aren't respected—whether by the leader or by fellow teammates—they don't feel they belong. They don't feel part of the team. Additionally, people feel singled out and ostracized when they're treated unfairly—especially in relation to how teammates are treated.

Self-Esteem

As we move upward in Maslow's Hierarchy, we next encounter self-esteem needs. Self-esteem needs are related to how we feel about ourselves and how others feel about us. Self-esteem needs include the need to feel confident, the need to have a sense of accomplishment, the need to have the respect of others, the need for some degree of status, the need to have autonomy, the need for responsibility, and the need to have a good reputation.

In order for these needs to be met, there must be a culture of mutual respect and positive communication. People must be granted sufficient autonomy to explore solutions in ways that will reflect their individuality. Work must be matched to skill sets in order for people to successfully complete their work in a creative, productive manner. Conversely, when skills and tasks are mismatched, it causes stress, mediocre results, and possibly the need for performance-enhancing solutions (as in drugs or excessive caffeine).

Self-Fulfillment

The final category of needs is self-fulfillment. Self-fulfillment needs include the need for personal growth, the need to work towards a meaningful purpose, and the need to have an impact beyond personal interests.

In order for these needs to be met, the opportunity for personal growth must exist. People must have the opportunity to explore possibilities and potential. The ability to make a difference must exist in order to give meaning to work.

Of course, the critical issue here is not simply understanding the range of needs people have, but appreciating that when those needs aren't met, disillusionment and disengagement occur. And although some needs are best met by the organization, the fulfillment of the majority of these needs falls squarely on the shoulders of the leader(s). The degree to which someone's needs are met by their leader is determined by 1) the quality of the leader's character (how they act), 2) how effectively they interact with people (how they interact), and 3) how well they guide the organization (how they guide).

How We Act (Self)

How well we conduct ourselves

A leader whose character causes his or her team to lose trust and respect cannot bring out the best in people. By clarifying and honing the values and behaviors that matter to us and then acting in a manner consistent with those values and behaviors, we establish our character to those around us. Here are the competencies related to how we act which determine how well we are able to bring out the best in people:

- **Show integrity**
- **Earn respect**
- **Be transparent and vulnerable**
- **Maintain a positive attitude**

How We Interact (Team)

How well we relate to people

The manner in which we interact with people plays a large part in determining whether we're trusted and respected by our team. It affects our ability to influence people and impacts the level of response we get from people. A leader who interacts with people in a manner, which minimizes them and demonstrates they don't value, respect, or trust them will alienate people, causing them to disengage. People who don't feel valued and respected become ambivalent. Here are the competencies related to how we interact that determine how well we are able to bring out the best in people:

- **Treat people like people**
- **Communicate effectively**
- **Treat adults like adults**
- **Resolve conflict**
- **Show appreciation and recognition**

How We Guide (Organization)

How well we guide the organization

The role we play in defining and establishing the future of our team and our organization is critical to bringing out people's best. A leader who doesn't provide the vision, inspiration, and growth an organization needs, creates an environment that lacks passion, purpose, and drive. Our ability to paint a picture of the future can inspire people, instill a sense of pride, and create the desire to be part of something meaningful. Here are the competencies related to how we guide that determine how well we are able to bring out the best in people:

- **Develop compelling initiatives**
- **Set clear expectations**
- **Develop people**
- **Be inspiring**
- **Be of service**
- **Lead appropriately**

In the next chapters, we'll explore the means to create a vibrant, engaged organization. We'll discuss what it takes to elevate character, interact with others more effectively, and guide the organization in a more meaningful way. We'll look at why each behavior matters and what things to do to bring out the best in people.

CHAPTER 3: HOW WE ACT (SELF)

How well we conduct ourselves

In this chapter, we'll discuss the competencies related to how we act. People determine what kind of person we are by observing how we act in various situations. Their assessment of us in everyday situations defines who we are in their eyes.

The competencies that relate to how we conduct ourselves are:

- **Show integrity**
- **Earn respect**
- **Be transparent and vulnerable**
- **Maintain a positive attitude**

Show Integrity

Do what you say you're going to do and be who you say you are.

Why It Matters

The importance of earning the trust of the people you lead is well accepted yet still remains an issue. Trust is earned through having integrity and is absolutely essential for keeping people engaged. A leader who lacks the trust of others has a difficult time influencing and inspiring them. It's not simply a matter of being honest, nor is it a matter of not being dishonest. Our integrity is reflected in what we do and who we are. People assess us by our words and actions over time (although a single negative event can change that opinion instantly). We don't earn trust by how we act during major events, but rather how we act in everyday situations. Our words and actions will carry more weight and have greater impact if we've earned the trust (and respect) of others in advance.

How we behave over time—our everyday actions and behaviors—defines who we are in the minds and hearts of those around us. The more people trust and respect us, the greater our ability to bring out the best in them. An associate of mine calls these "moments of apparent insignificance." This concept is very real and can be easily demonstrated.

Think back to your years in school. Do you remember something that someone said or did back then? Most all of us can recall some event or incident. I guarantee the other person doesn't know you remember! To them, their words or actions were insignificant. But to you (and no doubt others who heard or observed them), that event made an impression and to this day causes you to view that person in a certain way.

The level of trust and respect given a leader by his or her team determines—to a great degree—the lengths people are willing to go for them. A leader who has earned a high degree of trust and respect creates a loyal team. A leader who has earned trust and respect gains the ability to greatly influence the actions and performance of his or her team. And a leader who has earned trust and respect will be more easily and more quickly forgiven for mistakes they make. And we all make mistakes.

What To Do

Don't "try" to do things. Typical of a leader who lacks integrity is that he or she often *tries* to do things. In other words, someone who *tries* to do something gives themselves the option of not doing that thing. Someone who *tries* to show up on time often shows up late, rationalizing why they were late. Someone who *tries* to accomplish a task on time often doesn't, explaining their missed deadline with a reasonable excuse. And while no one will chastise them for this behavior, people learn that that leader is not dependable—they can't really be trusted to do what they say they will do.

Likewise, if someone claims, for instance, that a strong work ethic is important but then they don't work diligently, it demonstrates a lack of integrity. It shows they aren't who they claim to be. "Do as I say, not as I do," shows insincerity and a lack of integrity.

As Yoda said in the movie, *The Empire Strikes Back*, "Do or do not. There is no try." If you want to establish your integrity as a leader, don't *try* to do things or *try* to be a certain way. Either agree to do something or agree not to do it. Be a person who embodies a certain set of values or don't claim the importance of those values.

Act with integrity. Acting with integrity means doing what you say you will do and not committing to something you don't intend to do. Most people feel they do what they say they're going to do, but the truth is that we often view our actions through filters. An additional challenge with demonstrating our integrity is that we generally act and react out of habit and, as such, aren't very mindful of our words and actions. Here are a couple of practical examples of how to establish our level of integrity:

Show up to meetings on time. Although showing up late may not feel like a big deal, always showing up on time sends the message that you're a person of your word and that you value your team and their time. For example, we may call a meeting for 10 am but show up at 10:05. We'll always have a reason for being late, and we always feel the reason is valid. Perhaps we're in the habit of showing up late, or maybe our tardiness was unavoidable, caused by someone or something else demanding our time. People may be used to our lateness, but it doesn't make it right. In fact, being late may have very little impact on whether people view us as having integrity, but the impression it makes when you're always on time can have a significant impact. When a leader is always on time, people learn that they are a person of their word. You establish yourself as someone who means what you say and someone who can be counted on.

Of course, sometimes we're unavoidably detained or delayed. In the event that circumstances delay you, calling ahead to announce that you're going to be late also shows integrity because it demonstrates that you take your commitments seriously. It's considerate and makes a strong statement about who you are. The impact those actions have on establishing your integrity is immeasurable.

Only take on tasks you intend to complete. Be honest with yourself and with others. A person of integrity either follows through on their commitments or declines to take on the commitment. But they don't *try* to do them. Committing to a deadline creates an opportunity to demonstrate your integrity. Regardless of the importance of the task, fulfilling your commitment on time cements your level of integrity in the minds of others. Only when you have consistently demonstrated that you are a person of your word can solid trust be established.

Act in integrity. Acting in integrity is slightly different than acting with integrity. It's about how we conduct ourselves and it relates to the values we claim matter to us. It starts with gaining clarity about the values and behaviors you feel best define you. These are things like honesty, respect for others, integrity, caring, effective communication, and business ethics. There are no right or wrong answers. They are simply the values you most want to be known for.

Once you have clarity about those values, strive to live by them and demonstrate them in your words and actions on a consistent basis. A person who acts in integrity does not compromise their values and principles. Acting in integrity means that if we say that treating others with respect matters, we are always respectful of others—regardless of the situation or the person's position. It requires us to be mindful in every one of our actions, interactions, and reactions. Acting in integrity means that if we say that honesty matters to us, we are honest—regardless of the situation. If you purchase a cup of coffee or pay for a meal and you receive more change than you should, you return the overage—even if you are the only one who will know. If you say that work/life balance matters, then you go out of your way to strike that balance—not only for you, but for the people you lead as well. A person who acts in integrity embodies their values in all they do.

Earn Respect

Everyone feels they have something to contribute. Pay attention to them.

Why It Matters

Respect, like integrity, is one of those things that no one argues against. Yet, not every leader earns the respect of his or her team. If a leader wants to be influential and inspirational and bring out the best in people, he or she needs to have the respect of those they lead. There is a big difference between acceptance and respect. Just because someone responds to our requests doesn't mean they respect us. A request from someone who isn't very well-respected generally yields a basic performance of duties, with the results being mediocre. In contrast, the same request from a well-respected leader generates extra effort and tends to produce more than acceptable results.

If a leader has the respect of those around him or her, they possess a greater ability to persuade people to their point of view. When a leader lacks the respect of the team, their ideas and opinions won't be respected either. Most of their ideas or suggestions will be dismissed or regarded with skepticism.

Additionally, similar to the dynamic that exists relative to integrity, a well-respected leader who makes a mistake is almost always forgiven. But in contrast, when a leader who has not earned respect makes a mistake, people often see the mistake as confirmation that the leader doesn't deserve respect.

Stop pretending to value people. The quickest way to lose the respect of others is to regard them in a way that demonstrates you don't respect them. People feel they're not respected when they're spoken to in a manner that either minimizes them or makes them feel they and their ideas are being dismissed.

Give people your full attention. We show respect to people when we give them our full attention. It demonstrates that we care about their ideas and concerns and that we feel what they have to say is valuable. Conversely, we make people feel that we don't value them when we don't give them our full attention. Have you ever gone into someone's office to speak with them and had them multitask while you offered your thoughts and perspectives? How did it make you feel? Most people feel that the other person considers what they have to say no better than—or even less important than—the emails the other person is reading and responding to. Or have you ever had someone take an unimportant phone call in the middle of a conversation with you? If you've ever experienced that, you know it sends the message that you are relatively unimportant and fairly irrelevant. And how about the leader who takes calls or responds to texts during a team meeting? It demonstrates to everyone in the room just how little the leader values and respects them.

Ask for input. We show that we respect people when we solicit input from them on matters that will impact them, or in which they have expertise or experience. People want to be respected for their ideas and their efforts. Listen to them and value their perspectives— regardless of whether you agree with them or not. We make people feel that we don't value them when we either don't ask for their input or don't listen to what they have to say. Have you ever had a leader—or a company—establish a new policy that didn't address an issue the team had, or worse, had a negative impact on progress or productivity? And they developed the policy without soliciting input from the team? It makes most people feel that the leader doesn't care about the team's concerns and that the opinions of the team are irrelevant. Actions like that convey the message that the leader feels the members of the team have poor judgment or nothing of value to contribute.

Or have you ever had a leader ask for input or concerns and then completely ignore everything said? They end up doing exactly what they wanted to do in the first place. Actions like that also demonstrate that the leader doesn't respect his or her team and feels that by appearing to care, people will feel valued. Let's face it—most people see right through this, and those actions have just the opposite effect. People lose respect for the leader because of their efforts to create the false impression of caring about the team's opinions.

Criticize in private. We make people feel that we don't value them when we interact with them in a disrespectful manner. When a leader belittles someone—whether in private or in public—they devalue them and show them disrespect. When a leader chastises someone in public, they show them no respect. Actions like these embarrass the individual and harm their self-esteem. But just as harmful is the negative effect these actions have on the entire team. These actions demonstrate that the leader is uncaring, insensitive, and willing to turn on any team member—hardly the way to bring out the best in people.

Respect is earned by having integrity. People respect someone who can be counted on. They respect someone who does what they say they will do, acts in accordance with their values, and does not compromise their principles. Clearly, integrity is an essential trait for effective leadership.

Have passion, purpose, or conviction for something. People admire and respect a person who is passionate about something or is moved to action in pursuit of a worthy cause—regardless of whether they share that same passion. People are attracted to us and respond to us based on who we are, and having passion and purpose helps influence how people see us.

> *Years ago, when I first started my business, I built up my clientele almost exclusively through public speaking. I spoke to various groups and gave the same talk throughout the year. It was a talk on leadership—a topic I was and still am passionate about. At the end of each talk, I invited people in the audience to come up to me afterwards if they were interested in working with me as a business/executive coach. All in all, I had over 200 people ask to work with me. Here's the interesting question... "How many of them wanted help with becoming a better leader?" The answer may surprise you. (I know it surprised me.) You might expect all of them did, or at least the majority did. **Only one person wanted help with becoming a better leader!** The others wanted help with things like marketing, systems, profitability, and career development. One person even wanted my help in finding a new relationship! After reflecting on what was happening, it became clear to me. People were attracted to me because of my passion.*

Most people are not passionate about anything in their life. Henry David Thoreau wrote, "The mass of men lead lives of quiet desperation." Consequently, a leader who is passionate about something—anything—becomes a magnet, attracting those around him or her. They admire and want to be associated with him or her. In short, people respect a leader who is passionate.

Demonstrate fairness. When a leader treats people fairly, their team respects them. If a leader shows favoritism, the people around him or her lose respect. When a leader singles someone out for harsh treatment, it is viewed as arbitrary and unfair. It is it is essential that each member of the team be treated equally. Be consistent in your dealings with members of your team. It demonstrates that the leader values each of them.

Be Transparent and Vulnerable

Admit your mistakes—both past and present.

Why It Matters

If a leader truly wants to bring out the best in people, he or she must be transparent and vulnerable. That doesn't mean they tell everyone everything about themselves. Nor does it mean they need to be an emotional open book. No...it's a bit different than that.

It's about helping people understand why things are happening and why certain decisions are made. And it's about allowing people to see that you—as a leader—make mistakes and don't have all the answers. As we discuss why and how transparency and vulnerability matter, it will become increasingly apparent how to be more of each.

Transparency

"I think the currency of leadership is transparency. You've got to be truthful. I don't think you should be vulnerable every day, but there are moments where you've got to share your soul and conscience with people and show them who you are, and not be afraid of it."
–Howard Schultz, CEO of Starbucks

Most people don't like surprises—especially those which may affect their life and their future. When a leader remains silent on decisions made or actions taken, you can be assured that people will invent stories about why those decisions were made or actions were taken. They don't simply accept things, and they won't simply trust that the company and its leaders are looking out for the well-being of the people who work for them.

A leader may have concerns about how people will react to bad news or unpopular decisions, but there are a number of truths that should override those concerns. The first truth is that the fear of the unknown is generally greater than the fear that may come from receiving some unpleasant news. The second truth is that the stories invented in the absence of an explanation will almost always be inaccurate and less positive than the truth, leading to widespread rumors and unnecessary discomfort. When there is a lack of transparency, people will generally conclude that there is an ulterior motive, which leads to feelings of mistrust.

The third truth is that people really do want a leader who is forthright. They want to be led by someone who is honest and will work for their future. People want to know that one way or another, things will be OK. The fourth truth is that people don't want to feel excluded. The need to feel that we are in the know is a universal need. And the fifth truth regarding transparency and vulnerability is that people can handle the truth. Everyone knows that things don't always go as planned, and they understand that circumstances can cause difficult situations. When a leader is transparent and forthright about a situation, it allows the team to come together and address whatever is going on. A great example of how being transparent can make a difference is the story of how Jack Stack turned around the fortunes of the Springfield ReManufacturing Corp.

The company had come in existence through a <u>highly</u> leveraged buyout of the factory by a group of its managers. Although they all relished the idea of owning a company, the reality was that the business was in an extremely tenuous position. The slightest bump in the road would cause the business to close. Stack's course of action was to let all the employees—over 100 of *them—know just how precarious their situation was. He shared the company's financial position on a regular basis, helping everyone understand where the company stood and what had to happen to succeed. The result? Over the next 10 years, revenues climbed to almost $100 million and their stock price rose from $0.10 a share to $18.60! People would rather know what's going on and help drive success than be kept in the dark and live in uncertainty.*

Transparency and vulnerability also make a leader more relatable. When a leader is relatable, people respond more positively and with greater conviction. Being transparent and vulnerable is not only about allowing people to know what you're thinking but how you're feeling as well.

Not long ago, I had an executive as a client who was bright, experienced, and hard working. But he had a challenge. He found it difficult to allow people to read his emotions. He felt the need to appear unemotional when talking to members of his team. He didn't feel the need to project that he was happy or excited or annoyed or upset. He always interacted with people wearing an expressionless poker face. The consequence was that people couldn't relate to him. And because they couldn't, his ability to influence and to bring out the best in people was severely hampered. Additionally, he was unable to share his vision effectively, build buy-in, or inspire people. Only by opening up and becoming more human could he have the impact he wanted and needed.

Vulnerability

"The hardest thing about being a leader is demonstrating or showing vulnerability.... When the leader demonstrates vulnerability and

sensibility and brings people together, the team wins." –Howard Schultz, CEO of Starbucks

Leaders have vulnerabilities. We all do. And although most of us would prefer that others not know about those vulnerabilities, revealing at least some of them allows us to be more relatable—more human. When people better relate to us, the things we say and do have a greater impact. When we reveal that we're not perfect or all-knowing, it demonstrates that we don't have a big ego and that we don't feel superior to everyone else. Being vulnerable enhances our ability to bring out the best in people.

The dynamic related to vulnerability and relatability is an interesting one. A great example of its impact on people was illustrated by the lack of success (and subsequent success) of the Superman comic book.

Superman, the comic book hero, was created in 1933. And although people enjoyed his adventures, the comic never reached blockbuster status. Up until 1943, Superman was invincible. And then in 1943, the concept of kryptonite and Superman's vulnerability to it was introduced. With the introduction of a vulnerability—kryptonite—people found the character to be more human. Consequently, he became more relatable. It was this aspect of vulnerability that caused people to root for the superhero to overcome adversity.

In spite of the fact that allowing people to see some of our vulnerabilities can be a great asset in leadership effectiveness, many leaders are still reluctant to admit or reveal or acknowledge any vulnerability. They fear they'll be viewed as weak or incompetent if they allow themselves to be vulnerable or allow people to see that they don't have all the answers. Besides that, there's often a fear that they'll be taken advantage of. Nothing could be further from the truth. When we allow people to see we have vulnerabilities, it not only shows that we're real but also that we're self-confident. Everyone appreciates that it takes courage to admit a vulnerability.

Think back to leaders you've worked with in the past. When a leader admitted they didn't have all the answers, did you think more or less of him or her? Most people admire someone who admits they don't know everything. When someone asks for *your* help, do you think less of them because they didn't have an answer? No. We generally think that smart people are clear about what they know and about what they don't know. Additionally, when a leader goes to someone for help, it demonstrates that they value, trust, and respect that person.

What To Do

Don't pretend to have all the answers. A leader who always claims to have all the answers is viewed as someone with a big ego. People know that no one has all the answers, so the leader comes across as defensive and as someone who lacks confidence. By not seeking advice and guidance from others, they also send the message that they don't value or respect the people around them.

Admit your mistakes. One of the most effective means of influencing others is to be the kind of person who admits the mistakes they've made. First of all, it makes us more relatable—because everyone knows that everyone makes mistakes. Someone who doesn't admit mistakes is suspect. Secondly, we all know that we learn more from our mistakes than from our successes. It helps people understand how and why we've gained the insights and wisdom we have. People will lack confidence in a leader's judgment if that leader claims to be free from mistakes.

Show why as well as what. Help people understand what is going on and why it's happening. A leader who doesn't share his motives or the company's motives with his or her team ends up keeping people in the dark—and no one likes being kept in the dark. Help them understand the motivations behind the decisions being made and the actions being taken. Trust that people can handle the truth. When people are clear about what's really happening, they are better able to overcome adversities and rise to the occasion. When we trust people to deal with the realities of a situation, we're treating them as adults and as professionals. Don't hide the *why* from people. It never turns out well.

Share your journey and your challenges. When people come to know where you've come from and the challenges you've faced, you become more real. It helps people appreciate who you are today and how you came to be that way. Don't take yourself too seriously. People who appear self-important aren't taken seriously. Don't be afraid to share some fears or insecurities. We all have them, and letting people know about some of them helps us to be more relatable.

Communicate personally. Transparency and vulnerability need to be communicated in person and not impersonally via things like email, texts, or memos. It's our sincerity that helps convey who we are. And don't just communicate to direct reports. Help people at all levels—from senior leaders to front line professionals—get to know you and the reasons behind events. You can accomplish this in a practical manner by walking around and being visible or by conducting monthly lunches, inviting people from throughout the organization. It's a great forum for exchanging ideas and sharing information.

Ask for help. A leader who leads in isolation alienates his or her team. When you ask for help, you elevate the value and self-esteem of those around you. Smart leaders surround themselves with smart people and then take advantage of those valuable resources.

Maintain a Positive Attitude

Feed yourself with positive input.

Why It Matters

Attitude plays an interesting role in our ability to bring out the best in people. There are two different dynamics at play that make attitude maintenance so important. The first dynamic relates to how our attitude affects our perception, our reality, our thinking, and our emotions. The second dynamic relates to how our attitude affects our team.

No one is against having a positive attitude. It's kind of like mom and apple pie. There's nothing to be against. Yet we all know people with a negative attitude. But here's the interesting thing: no one views himself or herself as negative! People who take a negative view of things consider themselves to be "realistic."

Our attitude affects the reality we experience because our reality is colored by how we perceive things, and our perceptions are altered by our attitude. Positive people tend to view challenges as speed bumps—obstacles to be overcome. In contrast, negative people tend to see these challenges as reasons why something can't be accomplished. While it's true that some things can't be changed or overcome, it is rare that there isn't a way around, over, or through most obstacles. Most great achievements initially appeared to be unrealistic—until the solution was found.

Back in the early days of the automobile, Henry Ford had a vision for improving a car's engine design. He wanted to find a way to cast the V-8 automobile engine as a single block. All the industry experts said that it couldn't be done. However, Henry

Ford was determined and assembled a great team of engineers. They worked for six full months but had no success. But Ford was a leader who had an optimistic attitude in spite of the fact that many people considered his quest to be unrealistic. He urged them to continue trying, and they continued to work for another six months, still without success. But Ford's determination and his team's sense of pride prevailed. Over the next months, they finally devised a means of casting a V-8 engine as one block—an innovation that revolutionized the auto industry forever.

A positive person tends to see possibilities and solutions where a negative person tends to focus on limitations and problems. Having a perspective that focuses on limitations and problems precludes bringing out the best in people. A positive, optimistic person tends to focus on finding ways to reach goals. A negative, pessimistic person focuses on reasons why things won't work and justifies giving up.

Another dynamic related to attitude is that people tend to seek out other people and other sources that support their point of view. A positive person will tend to associate with other positive people and will give greater weight to information that supports their perspective. Negative people will do the same thing. They'll seek out people and information that supports their view of a situation. In doing this, each type of person reinforces their belief, which in turn defines their reality.

A number of years ago I had a friend who became focused on the potential problems surrounding the change of the millennium (Y2K). As he began to obsess over the topic, the foretelling of upcoming disaster became his reality. The more he listened to radio talk shows, the more he accepted their topics as reality.

The more articles he read on the subject, the more he accepted those doomsday reports as reality. And the more websites he visited, the more he accepted their perspectives about Y2K as reality. By the end of December, he had stockpiled water and food and was pleading with me to move up to the mountains to escape the impending terrorist attacks, falling planes, food shortages, crashing cars, and lack of water. Of course, January 1, 2000, came and went without incident.

A positive attitude fosters positive emotions. Someone who is generally optimistic can handle setbacks and stressful situations better than someone with a pessimistic perspective. If our view of the world and our situation is generally pessimistic and negative, it creates a higher base level of stress. The consequence of this ongoing elevated state of stress is that when a new stress-causing situation arises, it causes us to feel much higher levels of stress, pushing us into an emotional state that is difficult to handle. In contrast, a person whose base level of stress is much lower can often take the new situation in stride without creating undo additional stress.

Elevated levels of stress adversely affect us in a number of ways. Prolonged stress can cause a multitude of health problems, ranging from heart disease and asthma to diabetes and headaches. Additionally, being in a state of high stress forces a fight or flight response. In times past, when physical danger was more prevalent and very real, it was critical—when faced with an imminent, life-threatening situation—to either fight to protect yourself or flee to protect yourself. There really wasn't time to sit and reason things out. Immediate action was called for. In order to facilitate this quick response, the brain cuts out the neo-cortex (the thinking, creative part of our brain) from the process, deferring to the amygdala (the emotional center of the brain) to control our actions. When this happens to us in times of high stress, our ability to think clearly, solve problems creatively, and communicate effectively becomes severely diminished. Remaining in a prolonged state of elevated stress is highly counterproductive—leading to poor thinking and misguided actions. Maintaining a positive attitude and lowering our levels of stress is critical to effective leadership and our ability to bring out the best in people.

Our attitude is contagious. A team's attitude, thinking, creativity, and actions are directly affected by the attitude of the team's leader. A team led by a positive, forward-thinking leader will act in a similar fashion. If the leader sees possibilities, the team will as well. A positive leader has a positive vision for the future, and their team will naturally buy into that vision. A positive leader helps the team be more creative in their solutions, which often leads to order-of-magnitude improvement. Conversely, a negative leader will slowly drag a team down. Negative thinking generally results in limited thinking, and limited thinking can, at best, result in only incremental improvement.

How does one turn a negative attitude into a positive one? The same way someone with a positive attitude maintains it. You need to take charge of what you put into your head. You need to eliminate the negative inputs, influences, and factors in your life and introduce positive ones. We're bombarded with messages throughout the day and night. Some of them are good and some of them are just plain bad for you. We get messages from family, friends, co-workers, radio, newspaper, TV, music, the internet, billboards, books, magazines, and any number of other sources. If you don't decide what goes into your head, then someone else will. You need to take control of what you feed your mind.

Stop reading and watching the news. This sounds extreme, but consider this: everyone acknowledges that the newspaper is mostly filled with negativity: murder, fire, war, disasters, etc. Stop feeding yourself with it! I haven't read the news nor have I watched the news in over 15 years. And yes, I remain unaware of the fires, murders, and car accidents that occur, but I am always aware of major events that take place around the country and around the world. You can't help but be informed about major stories one way or another. In this information age, it's difficult—if not impossible—to be unaware of major events. There's no need to go looking for news. And there's one more issue to consider. When you go to sleep at night, the mind starts processing the last things it was exposed to. So if you're hoping for a restful night's sleep, what's one of the most counter-productive things a person can do just before they go to sleep? *Watch the TV news!* Stop watching it.

Stop seeking the negative on the internet. The internet is a great resource for information, news, opinion, and entertainment. But one of the realities—and challenges—is that generally, there is no curation of content, meaning that anyone can write anything. Fiction can be portrayed as fact. Opinion can be portrayed as fact. And content can be one-sided and not even-handed. As with the example of my Y2K friend, if you seek out content that highlights a certain perspective, that perspective increasingly becomes your reality. If you dwell upon news and opinion that portray a dark world, your world becomes increasingly dark. Stop seeking out what you don't want.

Avoid negative people. If you want to begin shifting your attitude, it is essential that you distance yourself from those who take a negative or defeatist view of their life, their work, and their world. The more you expose yourself to negative input, the more it molds your attitude to match that view. If you want to adopt a different attitude about things, you need to be more selective about who you associate with.

Associate with positive people. Positive association is one of the keys to success. Positive association leads to creativity, partnerships, solutions, and bigger dreams. Mark Twain once said, "Keep away from people who belittle your ambitions. Small people always do that, but the really great make you feel that you, too, can become great." People who are naturally positive can help you see possibilities where none seemed possible. Positive people will offer perspectives different from your own, often triggering new ways of thinking and creative solutions. Positive people whose opinions you respect can act as a reliable sounding board, providing constructive feedback and guidance.

Start reading. It's often said that the books you read and the people you associate with determine where you'll be in five years. Where do you want to be? Start reading books about people you admire. Read personal growth books, books on success principles, and books about others who overcame challenges. Their stories are inspiring and offer hope about what is possible. Becoming inspired allows *you* to be a more inspiring leader, which helps you bring out the best in people. Their stories can help you see new possibilities and can help put a challenging situation into the proper perspective.

Start listening. Start using your windshield time as a time to learn and grow. Instead of mindlessly listening to music or talk on the radio, listen to audio books, podcasts, motivational CDs, or even music that lifts and energizes you. Create a mix of music that gets you and your attitude fired up for that next meeting, presentation, or prospect.

Do you know what happens when you listen to a motivational program or read an inspiring book? Nothing. Nothing happens immediately. But over time, those positive, thought-provoking perspectives and messages begin to have an effect. Over time, you'll discover that you're thinking in a new way. You'll find that your view of things has shifted, usually without even realizing that it shifted. You slowly transform your thinking, your emotions, and your perspective about the people and events around you.

CHAPTER 4: HOW WE INTERACT (TEAM)

How well we relate to people

In this chapter, we'll discuss the competencies related to how we interact. People determine what kind of person we are by observing how we interact with people in various situations. Their assessment of us in everyday situations defines who we are in their eyes.

The competencies that relate to how we interact with others are:

- **Treat people like people**

- **Communicate effectively**

- **Treat adults like adults**

- **Resolve conflict**

- **Show appreciation and recognition**

Treat People Like People

Things get managed. People get led.

Why It Matters

If you really want to bring out the best in people, you need to treat them like...well...people, rather than things.

At first, this seems fairly obvious and a competency everyone ought to be fairly good at. Or perhaps your inclination might be to dismiss this competency because it smacks of being touchy-feely, requiring a leader to be sympathetic to every emotional swing of every person you come in contact with.

But the concept of treating people like people is neither obvious nor soft. Instead, this concept provides for a high degree of accountability and yields strong business results. Let's begin by discussing what it means to treat someone like a thing and then expand on what it means to treat people like people.

We treat a person as a thing when we interact with them as if they were an object. Objects simply exist. They have no emotions, they don't think, and they have no judgment. Objects are resources, and resources get managed, optimized, utilized, and sometimes discarded. We relate to people as things when we take advantage of them. We regard someone as a thing when we see them as a problem. We are treating people as things when we consider them as tools to get what we want or simply to get the work done. When we interact with people without compassion, empathy, or understanding, we're relating to them as things.

Barbara knew this couldn't be good. She had been summoned to her boss's office and she could tell from the tone of his voice he wasn't happy. She wracked her brain to think of what she possibly could have done to deserve a reprimand but really couldn't think of a thing.

When she arrived at his office, she barely had time to shut the door before Jim unleashed a scathing attack on her, "What in the world were you thinking? How could you possibly have thought that ordering 100 cases of widgets was a smart idea?" Barbara began to explain her decision, but before she could get more than a couple of words out, Jim interrupted with, "I've been working to get inventory under control, and this really screws things up! You've really been careless with this, and it's going to create a real mess. From now on, I don't want you to order another thing without checking with me first." "I'm sorry," Barbara responded. "I won't let it happen again." "I hope not," Jim retorted. "Now get back to your office. I have a lot of work to do." Barbara left, feeling embarrassed and upset. She felt she had done the right thing and resented that she hadn't even been given the opportunity to explain herself.

Jim related to Barbara as a thing rather than as a person. It's not that Barbara didn't make a mistake. She did. It's not that Jim was wrong in being upset. He was justified. The issue here has nothing to do with the fact that a mistake was made and that it caused problems. The issue is with *how* Jim interacted with Barbara. He related to her as if she had no emotions, no forethought, and no judgment. In short, he related to her as a thing.

People respond to us based on who we are being rather than by what we do. The consequence of leaders treating people like things is that they'll get a response from people but not nearly the level of response they hoped for. In contrast, when we regard people as people, we recognize that people do have emotions. We recognize that people are trying to do good work. We recognize that everyone (including us) makes mistakes. And we recognize that everyone, regardless of position or title, has hopes and dreams, needs and desires, goals and aspirations, fears and stress, and strengths and weaknesses.

We can (and should) still hold people accountable and correct their mistakes even while caring about them and regarding them with compassion, empathy, and understanding. It's just that we need to do it in a way that treats them as a person, which consequently encourages them to be and do their best. When we are empathetic towards people, it allows us to appreciate any challenges they may be experiencing while still holding them accountable. Treating people like people isn't about accepting mediocrity. On the contrary. When we acknowledge people for who they are, it allows us to develop them to higher levels of success.

Treating someone as a person isn't so much about what we do or say. Instead, it's related to how we do or say those things. We can't disguise our true feelings. We communicate how we feel by the words we choose, the actions we take, and especially by *how* we do and say those things. And people respond to who we are, not what we do. By treating people as people, you gain their respect and their best effort.

A leader who treats people like people understands this and keeps it in mind as he or she leads. It allows us to not only address any issue in an effective manner but also keeps the other person fully engaged and productive. Coming from a perspective that people want to do a good job, that they don't intend to make mistakes, and that they aspire to something more will allow a leader to interact in a much more productive manner. This understanding affects *how* to go about leading, not w*hat to do* to lead.

A leader who regards people as people adopts an attitude of being of service to them. He or she helps them to be their best, to correct mistakes for the future, and is empathetic towards them and the feelings they are having.

Leaders who treat people like people bring out the best in them.

What To Do

Don't treat people like a problem or a nuisance. When we regard people in this manner, we minimize them and treat them as things. When people see a leader as uncaring about the challenges they have—whether their challenges are real or perceived—they lose respect for that leader and begin to disengage.

Don't interact in a dismissive manner. When we are dismissive with people, we demonstrate that we don't value them, their ideas, or their contributions. When people feel unappreciated, they feel undervalued and taken for granted. It makes them feel like a thing— easily replaced or discarded.

Don't adopt an insincere attitude. Although we may feel we are being clever by doing or saying the right things but are in fact insincere, people will generally see right through our façade. A leader who clearly feels one way but portrays him or herself in some different way is looked upon as lacking integrity—causing the leader to lose the trust of those around him or her.

Appreciate that people are trying to do a good job. Instead of reacting to mistakes by scolding people, find out why they did what they did and then help them improve their thinking, their judgment and their actions. Assume that people are trying to do their best and help them improve and grow. People will appreciate your interest in them and your desire to see them develop.

Remember that you make mistakes too. When we drop the illusion that we're error-free, we can more readily relate to the challenges others are having. When we relate our past missteps, it keeps people from being defensive about their own misguided actions. In helping people move past mistakes, we allow them to better take ownership of their actions, accept that their mistakes don't define them, and avoid mistakes in the future.

Care about people. Everyone has hopes and dreams, stresses and fears. When you care about people and what they're going through, you build loyalty and demonstrate sincerity. People want to be understood and they don't want to be judged. A leader who is non-judgmental can better hold people to a higher standard. People will generally rise to the occasion when they know they are understood and appreciated. Treating people like people brings out the best in them.

Communicate Effectively

Communicate the way others want to hear things.

Why It Matters

The ability to communicate effectively is essential for great leadership and for bringing out the best in people. Our ability to effectively share a vision relies on it. Our ability to influence and persuade depends on it. Our ability to effectively resolve conflict is in part directly related to our communication skills. It affects how well we lead a team and how effectively we delegate. It especially impacts our success as a presenter and the success of our sales efforts.

Alan and Ed arrived at Carl's office a few minutes past 10 am. Carl had called the meeting to get updated on the progress of the new marketing plan and he was already visibly impatient. Ed spoke first, asking Carl how his weekend was. Carl responded with, "Fine. Got a lot done around the house." Ed continued, "Me too. But Saturday night we had a blast! My wife and I went out to this great Italian restaurant and then saw that new action movie. Have you seen it yet?"

Carl, clearly less enthused than Ed, replied, "Ed, it sounds like it was a good time and I'd like to hear more about it later, but right now, I need to get the updates from the two of you. I only have about 15 minutes."

With that, Alan finally spoke up. "I've analyzed the market pretty thoroughly. First, I analyzed the current demand in the marketplace and then ran a regression analysis to project future growth. Then, I studied our competition and determined the likelihood of new competitors entering the market. After that,

I did my best to determine each competitor's market share and how much each product from each competitor contributed to their share. Then I analyzed how much of each competitor's share we'd need to capture in order to reach our goals. Then, of course, I ranked each one based on my estimate of the likelihood that we can actually achieve that piece of the market from each one. Look, it's probably easier for me to explain it using these charts and tables I've prepared."

Alan reached down to grab a stack of papers he'd brought with him. "Hold on, Alan," Carl insisted. "I trust your analysis of the market. Just give me the bottom line. What are your conclusions?" "Well," Alan replied, "as best as I can tell, we should be able to meet our goals if we come out with a campaign that drives sales of our premium products rather than our standard ones. I can show you why I think that." "Thanks, Alan, maybe later," Carl replied.

"Ed, how about your update?" Ed was excited to be able to show the creative work he and his team had been developing. "Well, Carl, we've been working hard to come up with really creative stuff. A couple of the guys came up with some pretty funny angles. It really is pretty imaginative. OK, so picture this. Two guys are standing next to our products and one guy says to the other, 'Hey Fred, have you heard the one about the giraffe and the kangaroo?'"

Carl held up his hand. "Ed, I don't have time to hear about it right now, but tell me this. Do you feel the campaign you're coming up with will drive sales of our premium product line?" Ed thought for a moment and responded it would. "Great! Here's what I'd like from both of you. Alan, prepare a one-page summary of your analysis and include a list of the initiatives we need to implement. Ed, I also need you to give me a summary of the marketing initiatives you feel we need to invest in. Can the two of you have that back to me by the end of the day?" They both nodded they could. "Great! Thanks for your hard work. I look forward to seeing what the bottom line is."

Talking and communicating are two different things. No doubt you've heard people talk and talk without really saying anything of substance or deliver their message in such as way that it was difficult to really comprehend the point they were trying to make. When it comes to communicating, there is a big difference between being right and being effective. Have you ever presented some information or a concept to someone only to see their eyes glaze over? They seem to drift off in their thoughts.

Effective communication is communication that delivers the right message in the right medium with the right style. When we deliver our message effectively, we help people see our point of view more easily and can better persuade them to our way of thinking.

Delivering the right message requires clarity of thought and clarity of purpose. It starts with being clear about the points you want to make. Often, this is more challenging than it sounds. The issue lies with the fact that we've given our ideas much more thought than the person or people we are going to speak to. If we deliver a message that doesn't make sense to the listener, it will be frustrating at best and be a poor reflection on us at worst. It is not sufficient to simply include all the points we want to make. We need to think through the process by which we want our listener(s) to move through in their thinking and perspectives. Deciding on exactly what points you want to make goes hand in hand with the second factor: clarity of purpose.

The effective crafting of a message is influenced by what it is that you're trying to accomplish with your message. A message that delivers information is different than one that is meant to persuade. A persuasive message is one which needs to incorporate an emotional component. Whether we're selling widgets or concepts, people buy emotionally. They may (and usually will) rationalize their decision logically, but the decision itself is made emotionally. That is the reason that focusing on benefits is more persuasive than focusing on facts. Benefits evoke emotions: pride, success, absence of pain, relief from stress, etc. The features or facts of our concept (or widget) become the rational justification for our decision. But the decision is made on an emotional level. Consequently, we need to help people feel the effects when trying to persuade people.

If you want your message to have the impact and effect that you'd like it to have, it must be delivered with the right medium. If the message is simply information that can't be misinterpreted and won't cause an emotional response, then written form is effective. Emails or memos are excellent media for disseminating information.

If, however, the information could be misinterpreted or if the information could trigger an emotional reaction, the written form is a very poor choice as a means of communicating. Additionally, if your message is not about information but rather intended to influence and persuade, written media are the least effective and can sometimes cause new issues to arise through misinterpretation.

When a message is meant to persuade or a message is emotionally charged, it is best delivered by spoken word. Speaking allows you to convey the underlying emotion of your message and gives context to your message. Delivering a message verbally allows you to help people feel the passion you have for your idea. It allows you to weave stories into your message, which helps listeners feel the points you're trying to make by painting a picture and evoking emotion.

But even when the right message is delivered with the appropriate medium, if that message is delivered in a style the listener has a hard time relating to, the full impact of your message will be lost. There are four social styles—analytical, commander, expressive, and stabilizer (A.C.E.S.)—and each style tends to think, act, interact, and make decisions in a different way. When we communicate in a style that matches our own primary social style, we generally only connect with a quarter of the people we speak with. If instead we communicate in a style which that matches the listener's primary social style, our message will be better received and our ability to influence elevated. If you want to bring out the best in people, communicate effectively.

What To Do

Don't react or respond impulsively. If you really want to be an effective communicator, it is imperative to express yourself well. It's almost impossible to compose your words and your thoughts well if you are impulsive with your communications. Have you ever received an email that upset or angered you, replied to it impulsively, hit send, and then regretted sending it? Either you thought of a better way to express what you wanted to say or you realized that your words could be misinterpreted? Don't respond to things impulsively.

Don't rely on written media to convey concepts or issues. Truthfully, most of us aren't especially good at conveying emotions, passion, or ideas in written form. When you attempt to do so, you run the risk of not communicating what you really want the other person to understand, or worse, having your intentions misunderstood. Emotions, passion, and ideas are best related verbally. Use written communication for the exchange of information and data.

Choose your words wisely. The art of influencing and persuading others relies on choosing the right words and using them in the right way. Semantics matter. Words often evoke emotions, so the use of the wrong word, or a less appropriate word, can bring forth an unintended emotion or no emotion at all. By practicing the art of expressing yourself in the best way possible, you'll be more successful at influencing people, causing them to change their perspective and bringing out the best in them.

Use the other person's social style when communicating. People prefer to be communicated with in a style that matches their natural manner of speaking. By learning how to read someone's social style and then adjusting the manner in which you communicate with them, you'll elevate your effectiveness immensely.

There are four social styles: analytical, commander, expressive, and stabilizer (A.C.E.S.). One of the easiest ways to gain insight into a person's style is to listen to how they express themselves. People will usually reveal their primary style in how they speak, the words they use, and what they talk about.

Analyticals are just that: very analytical. They're organized, detail minded, and somewhat idealistic. Analyticals also tend to be perfectionists. When it comes to their speech pattern, analyticals are generally serious, introverted, and soft-spoken. They typically speak in even tones with a deliberate, measured pace. They'll often use words like *information, facts*, and *details*. Because they tend to be private, they won't care to share much about their private life, and because they tend to be process oriented (as opposed to people oriented), they're not much into small talk and prefer, instead, to dive right into the issues at hand.

Commanders are natural leaders. They are high achievers, can be bold and assertive, and are often very competitive. When it comes to their speech pattern, commanders are generally direct, outspoken, and extroverted. They'll often ask for "the bottom line" or a summary of your points rather than the details. Because they are process oriented (similar to analyticals), they don't enjoy small talk and generally find it annoying. They'd prefer to get right down to business. Their speech is generally louder, faster, confident, and more to the point.

Expressives are people people. They're animated, cheerful, and enthusiastic. Expressives mix easily, are spontaneous, and often are playful. When it comes to their speech pattern, Expressives are generally bubbly, chatty and extroverted. They are less about process and more about people, and they'll speak in a manner that reflects their light-hearted nature. They won't take an interest in details, facts, or figures, but they'll focus rather on the general feel of things, and they'll get a sense of whether they like and believe you based on those feelings. Because they are people oriented, they often engage on a personal level, frequently incorporating humor. Their speech is generally louder and faster but more playful than a commander's style.

Stabilizers are relationship builders. You'll often see them as accommodating, considerate, and easygoing. Stabilizers are great listeners, patient, and soft-spoken. When it comes to their speech pattern, stabilizers are generally quiet, considerate, and non-confrontational. They'll use words that reflect their desire to help and their desire to keep things running smoothly, and they prefer to avoid conflict. Because they are people oriented, they need to connect on a personal level prior to diving into business matters. To Stabilizers, small talk allows them to connect with and better relate to others. Their speech is soft, slow, and mild mannered.

Use more stories and analogies to influence and persuade. One of the most effective means of changing a person's perspective and prompting them to action is through the use of stories and analogies. A well told story will cause people to imagine the consequence of your ideas. Stories can bring forth emotions that will support your cause. People buy emotionally, and you'll be far more successful when you help them feel the same enthusiasm you have. It's the reason that benefits are more persuasive than facts or features.

Using analogies can be an effective means of changing someone's perspective. Often, when we're trying to make a point and relate it to the person's specific situation, they can become defensive. However, by using an analogy, we remove the personal aspect from the point we're trying to make, thereby preventing those defensive walls from going up and leaving the listener open to hearing what we're saying.

Treat Adults Like Adults

Grant more autonomy.

Why It Matters

If you want to bring out the best in people, you need to treat adults like adults. Unfortunately, leaders often fall into the habit or pattern of treating adults like children. What constitutes treating adults like children?

When a leader micromanages people, he or she is treating them like children. When a leader regularly tells people what to do and how to do it, he or she is treating them as children. When a leader doesn't trust his or her team to follow through and act responsibly, he or she is treating them as children.

Why would a leader treat an adult like a child? It may happen for a number of reasons. The most prevalent reason stems from the flawed perspective that if people aren't told what to do, nothing will get done. It arises from the misguided belief that if people aren't managed, they will attempt to get away with whatever they can. It presupposes that people will do the least amount of work possible, doing just enough to keep from losing their job. That same kind of thinking would assume that unless someone more responsible is overseeing people, they will cut corners wherever possible.

Sometimes this behavior occurs because it is based on the example set by leaders from a person's past. If we don't have a better role model, we tend to model whatever we've been exposed to—even if it's poor leadership. And yet other leaders may treat people like children because they feel that the only way to get good work out of people is to manage them to his or her standards. Of course, this has just the opposite effect. Things get managed. People get led. When we manage people, it demonstrates a lack of respect and trust. Just as with children, when we treat people this way, it sends the message that we don't trust them to do what needs to be done and don't trust their judgment. When people feel they aren't respected and valued, engagement is lost. Hardly the way to bring out the best in people.

In order to treat people like adults, we need to eliminate the false perception that people will do as little as possible if left to their own initiative. The idea that people won't do a good job unless managed is simply wrong. Most people truly want to do the best job possible. Most people take pride in the work they do.

Daniel Pink, in his book *Drive*, discusses the power of granting autonomy. In situations where producing widgets is the result of a person's efforts, offering additional money may be an effective incentive for higher productivity. But in this day and age, when many people are earning a living with their mind, autonomy drives productivity and creativity.

The key to successfully granting autonomy is accountability, and the key to holding people accountable is becoming clear about just what it is you're holding them accountable for. When it's a task that we're talking about, the result we're holding them accountable for is fairly clear. However, when we're talking about holding someone accountable for a job or a position, the definition of what someone is being held accountable for is much more difficult to define, communicate, and measure. There may be quantitative aspects that can be readily defined, but as likely are important qualitative aspects that are much more difficult to define and hold someone accountable to.

Another aspect of treating adults like adults involves expanding the responsibility and authority of team members. This, of course, requires that a leader delegate effectively. People generally rise to new challenges, so delegating becomes a powerful tool for bringing out the best in people. Besides the obvious benefit of freeing up more of your time, delegating accomplishes two other important things: it helps people increase their value and expertise, and it demonstrates that you trust and respect the people you delegate to.

In order to delegate effectively, you first need to move past any issues standing in the way. You may be limiting yourself with the "I can do it better" syndrome. You know this kind of thinking. "If I ask someone else to do this, I'll just have to redo it anyway." If that happens, then either it's due to poor communication on your end or you have the wrong people on your team. Or you may feel that tasks and responsibilities are just too difficult to pass off or teach someone to do. You've seen this one, too. "It will take me longer to teach them how to do this than it will for me to do it myself." That may be so, but when you add up a year of doing it yourself compared to teaching it to someone one time, it's no contest.

Your ability to delegate effectively may be restricted by some very real and practical reasons, like having too few people (they're already overworked) or having the wrong people working for you (a fundamental issue that should be immediately addressed). However, barring those practical limitations, by practicing effective delegation, you'll bring out the best in people.

Of course, if your goal is to grant as much autonomy as possible, it is also necessary that people have the right tools, the appropriate skills, and the proper judgment to do their job effectively. Our job as a leader is to ensure we prepare people to do the best job possible. We'll talk more about this aspect of leadership in the next chapter.

What To Do

Don't micromanage. Micromanaging is frustrating and stressful for everyone—including you. It's counterproductive because it shows you don't trust people's abilities or judgment. If you feel the need to micromanage, try looking in the mirror. The issue lies with trying to manage people instead of leading them.

Don't assume people can't be trusted. Let go of the belief that people will try to do the least possible and replace it with a belief that people are professional and want to do the best job possible. If someone isn't doing a great job, look for another explanation. It may be that you haven't communicated effectively. It may be that they need additional tools or skills. Or it may be that they are in the wrong position for their natural skill set.

Grant more autonomy. Practice giving people more leeway over how they complete their work. Is productivity really determined by how many hours someone sits at their desk? Is it really determined by which hours they work? Could there be more than one way to get a job done? Could someone actually have a better solution or approach than yours? Assume people are professional and responsible and then hold them accountable for getting results.

Gain clarity about exactly what you expect from people. This can be a challenging task and requires you to really think about what you want to hold each person accountable for. It's not about what you want them to do. Instead, it's about the results you want and the parameters within which they need to operate. Results are more important than the hours someone works. Results are more important than the specific tasks they complete. And the values and behaviors that govern their actions are as important as the results they get. Things like honesty, ethics, respect, and collaboration are essential. In other words, the ends don't always justify the means. How they get results matters.

Delegate effectively. Effective delegation starts with choosing the right tasks to delegate. A good rule of thumb to start with is that any task that doesn't require judgment is a good candidate for delegation. As your confidence in someone's judgment grows, more important tasks can be delegated. The next step is to select the right individual for the task. You should identify which people have the natural talents needed for the task and then ascertain whether they would like to take on the assignment. The person with the right skills and the greatest enthusiasm will do the best job. Make sure they have the right tools and knowledge, and make sure they are comfortable coming to you for guidance and advice if they need some. And finally, ensure accountability. It is essential you have an agreed upon timeframe and a sense of whether the task is urgent or critical. The more urgent or critical, the more you need to check in on the progress of the project and ascertain whether any course corrections need to be made.

Resolve Conflict

Change people's perspectives.

Why It Matters

Effectively resolving conflict is essential for bringing out the best in people. Resolving conflict not only impacts the individuals with whom the conflict exists but the entire team as well.

No one relishes conflict. It usually causes anger, anxiety, and stress; is often frustrating; and at the very least, drains our energy. But there's no avoiding it. Conflict may occur with someone we report to, someone who reports to us, a peer, a vendor, or a client. The bottom line is that it's going to happen and we need to master the ability to resolve it effectively. If left unresolved, disillusionment begins, productivity drops, stress rises, and people start to disengage.

When conflict arises, there are several courses of action we can consider. One course of action is to do nothing and tolerate the conflict. Unfortunately, by not dealing with the situation, you end up perpetuating a number of counterproductive dynamics. You end up expending valuable energy by tolerating an unsatisfactory situation. It affects your attitude, your thoughts, and your productivity. Additionally, in your attempt to shield or isolate yourself from this person, they end up feeling neglected and unappreciated. When that happens, they tend to *check out,* becoming complacent and apathetic—simply going through the motions at work.

There's one other negative dynamic that exists when we tolerate conflict. Although it may feel like the issue is between the two of you; in fact, a difficult person affects your entire team, as will be evidenced by the people who'll come forth voicing their relief once the difficult person is gone. Tolerating conflict is not a very fruitful course of action.

Another course of action could be to let the parties try to deal with the situation themselves. This course of action generally doesn't work very well either. After all, if either of the parties was adept at conflict resolution, the conflict would already have been resolved. A festering conflict typically gets worse over time and begins to spread, affecting those around the parties. People often begin to take sides, dividing the team into factions and undermining teamwork and collaboration.

A third option is to resolve the conflict by telling the person or people to stop being difficult and to get along. Of course, this approach isn't effective because 1) it treats adults like children, 2) each party feels they are in the right, and 3) it simply causes them to harbor their feelings internally and not display them outwardly. The result is that although the appearance of resolution exists, so do all the negative consequences of a festering conflict.

Several things need to happen for conflict to get resolved. First, we need to prevent the conflict from escalating any further. Then we need to deescalate the conflict in order for each party to hear the other person and be open to other perspectives. And finally, we need to address the issue underlying the conflict.

One of the best ways to keep a conflict from escalating any further is to acknowledge that it exists. By acknowledging the conflict, each party stops pretending it doesn't exist and demonstrates that there is an underlying intent to resolve things. By not acknowledging a conflict, it sends the message that you either don't care that is exists or don't respect the other party enough to address their concerns.

A simple, yet effective, strategy for acknowledging a conflict and keeping things from escalating is to state the obvious. By simply stating your awareness that the conflict exists, you give validity to each side and open the door to the possibility of fruitful discussion.

The next step towards resolving a conflict is to remove or set aside any issues exacerbating the situation and then lay the groundwork for a resolution. Issues causing heightened feelings of conflict may include the physical location of the discussion, the presence of another person, the intermingling of personalities and issues, and the use of generalizations or exaggerations. Each of these issues is easy to address and must be addressed for any resolution to occur.

If location is an issue, have the discussion on neutral ground. Try meeting over lunch or at a coffee shop. If the presence of some other person adds to the conflict, prevents resolution, or may cause a loss of face, meet with each party privately. Often, the issues around a conflict can't effectively be examined and addressed if they are colored by someone's feelings towards the other party. Separate the personalities from the issues so they can be isolated and discussed. And finally, the issues many times are not as bad as they appear to be. In order to have a productive conversation about the issues, it is important to put them in the proper perspective by eliminating generalizations and exaggerations.

Once you've successfully kept the conflict from escalating and reduced the anxiety and intensity around the conflict, you can more effectively address and resolve the real issues. Underlying the strategies for successful conflict resolution is the reality that everyone feels they have a valid perspective, everyone wants to feel valued, and no one wants to be wrong or lose face.

In order to effectively resolve conflict, you need to understand why conflicts arise. Clearly, conflict can arise from any number of reasons. Most often, conflict occurs as a result of poor communication, unmet expectations, a difference in perceptions, a difference in priorities, mistakes, or fear. Therefore, the key to resolve conflict effectively is to uncover which of these reasons underlies the conflict and then address those reasons.

A leader who is adept at conflict resolution understands this and empathizes with the other person. They get the parties to commit to reaching a resolution. He or she *assesses* the other person and their position instead of *judging* them. And an effective leader strives to understand the other party's perspectives and their motivations.

The most effective means of understanding where another person is coming from is to ask questions. Asking good questions not only allows the parties to explain the issues and express how they feel about those issues, but—with skillful questioning—also uncovers why they feel the way they do. Once you understand why they feel the way they do (their motivations), you can more easily see their side of the disagreement and acknowledge and validate their point of view.

By successfully demonstrating you understand and value the other person and their perspectives, you can resolve conflict, restore harmony, and bring out the best in people.

What To Do

Don't tolerate drama or bad behavior. Don't avoid dealing with conflict. By ignoring a conflict, it suggests you don't care about the conflict or the people involved. Tolerating a conflict is demoralizing for the individuals involved and for the entire team. The effects of conflict are never limited to just the individuals involved. Although avoiding dealing with a conflict may feel like it is a good way to avoid aggravation and anxiety, allowing it to fester almost always leads to a much worse situation down the road.

Don't view the other party as an opponent. Adopting a win-lose approach generally backfires. While you may win the battle, you will usually lose the war. When a person feels they've been defeated, they often resent it and will look for an opportunity to undermine you at a later date. Instead, adopt a cooperative approach and work collaboratively to find a win-win resolution.

Focus on issues rather than people. The strength of a team relies on having people with different perspectives and different personalities. Don't allow differing styles and personalities to cloud the real issues. Acknowledge the personality differences, but move the conversation to a discussion of the issues. Only by taking the personalities out of the equation can a solution be found.

Focus on the specific issues rather than generalizations or exaggerations. Although a situation may feel like it *always* happens or affects *everyone*, it is rarely the case. Work to ascertain the true extent of the issues under discussion. The closer to the truth you get, the easier it is to resolve the matter in an effective way.

Strive to understand the person and their perspectives. The key to changing someone's perspective is to understand why they feel the way they do. Ask questions to determine their position. Then ask more questions to understand why they feel the way they do—their motivations. Once you have a clear understanding, you'll be better able to offer other perspectives and influence them to adopt a different way of thinking.

Show Appreciation And Recognition

Be grateful for people's efforts and achievements.

Why It Matters

In order to bring out the best in people, they need to feel valued. And in order for people to feel valued, a leader must show appreciation for their efforts and recognize them for their accomplishments.

Have you ever worked especially hard on something—putting in extra hours, sacrificing time with family or friends, and coming up with a clever approach—only to have your work go unnoticed or unappreciated? The fact that you can recall an incident like that speaks to the effect taking people's work for granted has on them. It's fairly self-evident that being taken for granted is disheartening, but it frequently happens in the business world nevertheless.

Why do some leaders seem to take people's efforts for granted? A leader may overlook someone's efforts and accomplishments for several reasons. Sometimes the leader is the kind of person who regards people as tools to get the work done (regards people as things) and therefore doesn't feel compelled to acknowledge or praise their work. This of course, is a poor perspective and discourages best effort.

Some leaders adopt the attitude that people are paid to do a job and therefore the payment of a salary is sufficient appreciation and recognition for their work. While it's true that people have an obligation to do good work in exchange for fair pay, people are still people. They have emotions, pride, fears, self-esteem, and a desire to please. There is a significant difference between someone who does a good job and someone who is engaged, enthused, and devotes discretionary time and effort to a project. The idea that people have a business life and a personal life is false. People have one life, and how much of it they devote to business endeavors is up to them. With only compensation as the reward for their work, people will generally only do what is required of them.

A third reason a leader may not show appreciation or offer recognition is that they get caught up in their own efforts and sacrifices and don't notice the efforts and sacrifices of others. It's an easy trap to fall into and can make a leader blind to the efforts of those around him or her. Showing appreciation and recognition to others while we ourselves are striving to achieve takes an extraordinary and self-aware leader.

Regardless of the reason behind a leader not showing appreciation or offering recognition, the results are the same: average performance from their team.

Both recognition and appreciation are important but are given for different reasons. The distinctions are important to understand. Recognition is typically offered as a reward and acknowledgement for accomplishments. Public recognition boosts a person's stature within an organization and enhances their self-esteem.

Appreciation, on the other hand, is generally shown in response to the effort someone makes, rather than an accomplishment. Sincere appreciation is generally spontaneous and heartfelt—given from one person to another. When we let people know we appreciate their efforts, it communicates that we're grateful for their efforts and that we respect and value them. The impact of showing appreciation is immediate and long-lasting. When a person's efforts and sacrifices are sincerely appreciated, self-esteem rises, engagement rises, and loyalty rises.

Recognition and appreciation each have a place in making a difference with people, but appreciation's impact is stronger than recognition's and has a more positive impact. Additionally, the opportunities for showing appreciation are more numerous and more frequent than those that deserve recognition.

In order to bring out the best in people, get into the practice of showing sincere appreciation.

What To Do

Don't take people for granted. Even if *you* feel people are simply doing the work they're paid to do, it's how *they* feel that should guide your actions. If someone expresses their feelings about the effort and sacrifices they've made, don't take those efforts for granted. Show them you appreciate the work they did.

Don't be insincere in your appreciation. People see right through insincerity, so being insincere sends the message that you don't respect or value them. It causes a loss of respect and trust, which leads to disillusionment. Understand that each of us has different skills and different capacities. These differences lead to differing feelings regarding the amount of effort and sacrifice being made. If it becomes clear that someone feels they've gone above and beyond in their efforts, show sincere appreciation.

Avoid recognition programs. Recognition programs offer guidelines under which a person is entitled to receive some form of recognition. On the surface, this seems like a reasonable approach that would encourage best effort. But there are two fundamental problems with recognition programs. The first problem is that a structured approach becomes impersonal and somewhat insincere. Recognition ends up bestowed upon someone simply because the program dictates that recognition be offered, not because it's especially noteworthy. The second problem is that recognition is offered to acknowledge a person's achievement rather than their effort. And the reality is that much of what people achieve on a day-to-day basis is routine and not especially noteworthy.

Show sincere appreciation. Most people want to be appreciated for their efforts more so than for their accomplishments. Appreciation is generally personal and heartfelt, given from one person to another. And it's often spontaneously shown as a response to the effort someone put into completing a task. It is an expression of gratitude for someone's effort, and its impact is immediate and long lasting.

Telling someone you appreciate their effort in completing a project over the weekend has a far greater impact than offering a token of recognition for the end result. Plus, the degree of appreciation expressed is generally in direct proportion to the effort or sacrifice made by the person.

Offer recognition on an as-needed basis. Although receiving a reward as recognition for accomplishment is welcomed, studies have shown that once rewards become expected, they no longer motivate and often produce declining results. When someone achieves something of note, offer recognition in the form of something that is meaningful to them. Many people are not motivated by nor do they feel gratified by receiving money. Instead, recognizing them for their accomplishments by offering something that shows you understand what matters to them is far more meaningful. It may be a fully paid trip for two to some destination or extra time off to spend with family. It might be a donation to a cause they are passionate about or could be a new set of golf clubs for someone who's an enthusiast.

CHAPTER 5: HOW WE GUIDE (ORGANIZATION)

How well we guide the organization

In this chapter, we'll discuss the competencies related to how we guide. People determine what kind of person we are by observing how we guide the organization in various situations. Their assessment of us in everyday situations defines who we are in their eyes.

The competencies that relate to how we guide the organization are:

- **Develop compelling initiatives**
- **Set clear expectations**
- **Develop people**
- **Be inspiring**
- **Be of service**
- **Lead appropriately**

Develop Compelling Initiatives

Develop initiatives that mean something.

Why It Matters

People do their best when they're inspired by and aligned with the work they're doing. When people are working on an initiative that matters to them, they're engaged and enthused. Why does a compelling initiative make such a big difference? An initiative with a purpose or a compelling reason provides meaning and value to people.

When you develop a strategic initiative that incorporates a compelling reason, you tend to bring out the best in your people. There are many notable examples of this dynamic in action.

One example is that of Zappos. Here's a company that lives and breathes its culture. All their initiatives revolve around providing the best customer service possible. They hire for that initiative, train for that initiative, empower for that initiative, and reward for it. They ensure that only people who are passionate about service become part of their team. Or consider Apple, who really isn't in the business of manufacturing or selling computers, iPods, iPhones, or iPads. Instead, they are in the business of creating solutions that enhance people's lives in an easy-to-use manner with elegant, beautifully designed products. It's a purpose that is easy to get behind and become passionate about. It's a key to their success. And the financial results for Zappos and Apple speak for themselves.

A compelling initiative can create a sense of pride among team members and can create focus, clarity, and a sense of urgency. Instilling pride has a myriad of benefits—quality of work and workmanship improves, creativity and innovation increase, collaboration is facilitated more easily, and people are willing to go the extra mile to do their best. A team or department instilled with a sense of pride will excel simply to prove to others that things can be accomplished that are otherwise thought impossible.

Let me illustrate the power of professional pride with a remarkable leadership story.

Mortgage lender Fannie Mae asked more than 550 employees to bring down, move, and start up more than 300 business applications. They had to unplug, wrap, and box 577 computer servers, lay more than 1.8 million feet of copper cable and 35 miles of fiber. Department employees were asked to do their day jobs all week and then throw themselves into this new task over 13 consecutive weekends, often pulling all-nighters on Friday evenings—without even the promise of extra pay.

They did it flawlessly, without a single interruption to the company's business. The leader of the initiative inspired them, fed them, and instilled a great sense of pride in them. She showed her appreciation by serving about 1,600 pounds of chicken wings to her crews for midnight snacking, Friday-night themed dinners, ranging from New England clambakes to down-home southern cooking, and full-blown Saturday morning breakfasts with pancakes, eggs, bacon, and sausage.

Whether an initiative is compelling or not relies on whether the underlying strategy is developed properly. Too often, we see companies looking to increase profits develop a strategy to bring them closer to where they want to be. Except the so-called strategy they develop is not really a strategy at all. It's just a goal. Or sometimes it's simply a platitude—a nice-sounding but meaningless statement.

Regardless of whether they develop a goal or a platitude, the results are always the same. The so-called strategy is never realized. No amount of encouragement, accountability, or table pounding will lead to achieving the desired results. Only a true strategy stands a chance of achieving significant results.

In order to develop a strategy that creates a compelling initiative, it is essential to understand the distinction among strategies, goals, tactics, and platitudes.

Let's dispense with platitudes right up front. Platitudes are nice-sounding phrases that accomplish nothing. A typical platitude might read, "We strive to be the recognized leader in our field and meet our customers' expectations of excellence." It gives no direction, isn't actionable, and addresses no particular issue.

Next, let's move on to goals and tactics. In order to effectively understand why goals and tactics aren't strategies, we need to first describe the essence of a strategy. In simple terms, a strategy offers a general direction an organization must move in order to address a specific problem or issue.

A goal, therefore, is not a strategy. It's just a metric to measure progress in the execution of a strategy. It has no emotional or inspirational component. It's simply a means of determining progress. A strategic-sounding goal might be, "Our strategy is to double revenues over the next three years." No matter how detailed the plan is to achieve it and regardless of the fanfare with which it is rolled out, this non-strategy is simply a goal to double sales—nothing more. Not only that, but the desire to double revenues is completely arbitrary: a figure pulled out of the air. In truth, the only people who will be enthused about this non-strategy are the ones who set the goal.

A couple of years ago, I was part of a team of executive coaches who worked with executives from a large, international company. The firm was getting ready to launch a major initiative whose goal was to significantly boost sales, tripling them over a five-year period.

They created a detailed plan that laid out what each division should focus on, listed the five areas to focus on to achieve the desired results, and rolled the initiative out across the globe with great fanfare and enthusiasm. In addition, they asked each division to develop their own strategies for improving results in each of the five areas. All in all, it was an exciting and ambitious goal. And of course, everyone was behind it 100%.

Except for one small issue. No one really cared about it other than the handful of executives who developed it. When you boil the initiative down to its essence, they were simply asking people to commit to tripling sales over a five-year period. Not very compelling.

The result? After the first year—the year when everyone was most focused on the initiative and enthusiasm was at its peak— sales were down! There had been challenges in the global economy, production delays, and branding issues. Instead of finding ways around the obstacles, people resigned themselves to sluggish results.

The irony is that the underlying impetus for the initiative was a worthy and compelling reason. The company had over the years become just like its competitors, slugging it out with undistinguished products and solutions. The driver for the initiative had been a desire to once again become the preeminent solution provider in their industry, setting themselves apart as the best and brightest. It would have changed how the company viewed itself and caused a surge in professional pride.

Of course, tactics are not strategies either. Tactics are the means by which a strategic initiative can be achieved. Tactics—like goals—have no emotion or energy behind them. They are simply the mechanics of how things will get done. A typical strategic-sounding tactic might be, "Our strategy is to increase the sales force by 20% over the course of this year." It's simply a statement of mechanics to achieve something. The problem is that that *something* is undefined and therefore the metric is viewed as arbitrary as well.

A good strategy, in contrast to platitudes, goals, and tactics, addresses an issue or problem and provides a direction for the company to move. It also provides the reason for the initiative, creating a desire to achieve it. By way of example, if the core problem is a product line that is not differentiated from the competition, the strategy might be, "Our strategy is to become known as the innovator in our industry by developing customized products and services." This is an initiative that people can get behind and strive to achieve.

When an initiative matters to people, they invest their discretionary effort in developing creative solutions and overcoming the inevitable stumbling blocks that present themselves. Accomplishing a meaningful initiative is personally and professionally fulfilling and usually involves stretching beyond our previous self-imposed limits. When you help people stretch and use their creative abilities, it brings out the best in them.

Don't set goals. Setting goals doesn't inspire or motivate anyone. Goals are simply the mileposts to gauge progress. This includes financial goals as well. Not only do financial goals only excite the shareholders, but better financial results should be the consequence of a well-developed, well-executed strategy, not the other way around. As the organization moves closer to fulfilling its initiatives and its destiny, the financial aspirations of the organization can't help but be met along the way.

Develop initiatives that mean something. There are a number of ways an initiative can be inspiring, compelling, and meaningful. Initiatives that aspire to excellence can be very effective. People take pride in accomplishing things that are challenging or position them as superior. A well-crafted initiative will cause people to become creative in their solutions and persistent in their efforts. Improved financial results are the byproduct of a meaningful strategy. Getting better numbers will never suffice as the strategy itself.

By creating initiatives that require people to improve and be better than they were or better than the competition, high engagement can be achieved. The best, most effective initiatives prompt people to *be* more, rather than simply *do* more. Here are some thoughts on the types of initiatives that accomplish that:

- **Initiatives that strive for excellence**
- **Initiatives that spur a team on to achieve the unlikely or difficult**
- **Initiatives that require creativity and ingenuity**
- **Initiatives that aspire to something that's never been done before**

- **Initiatives that make a difference in the lives of people**

- **Initiatives that elevate the team or the company to an elite status**

- **Initiatives that strive to do something better, easier, or faster**

Initiatives like those above cause people to take ownership of and pride in their work. They create focus, clarity, and a sense of urgency. In short, they help bring out the best in the people.

Set Clear Expectations

Clarify what you expect and what people expect in return.

Why It Matters

People do their best and are at their best when they're fully engaged. But people become disillusioned and increasingly disengaged whenever reality doesn't line up with their expectations at work. If you've hired the right people, they're excited to be at your company when they start and are prepared to be fully engaged. But this enthusiasm will wane if we don't clarify right up front what we expect of them and what they expect in return. When expectations aren't made clear, people expect what they imagine work will be like or they'll base their expectations on their past experiences from other organizations. Either way, the disconnect that occurs when expectations clash with reality is unfortunate and disheartening.

The alarm clock went off at 5:45 am, but Robert was pretty much awake anyway. It was the morning of the first day at his new job and his head was swimming with ideas, visions of contributing, and making a difference.

The drive to work was uneventful, but he was filled with anticipation and the time went fast. He took the elevator up to the marketing department and walked past cubicle after cubicle to the office of the marketing director. Filled with anticipation once more, he poked his head in to announce his arrival. The room was empty.

A bit discouraged, Bob turned around and scanned the room for someone to help him. He intercepted the first person to walk past him, a twentyish woman who seemed to be on a mission.

85

"Excuse me," Bob blurted out. "Do you know where Karen is?"
"Karen Peters?" she asked. "Yes, I'm Bob Peterson, the new marketing guy and I'm trying to find her." "No. I didn't realize we had hired someone new," she said. "I think she's in a meeting." "Do you know where my desk is?" Bob asked. "I'm afraid I don't," she replied. "Let's put you at Patty's old desk for now."

She walked him over to an empty cubicle on the other side of the room. "Make yourself comfortable, Bob. The coffee is in the break room and the restrooms are down the hall. I've got to run off to meet a deadline, but I'm sure Karen will be back shortly. Welcome to our family!" And then she turned and was gone.

Bob sat there feeling rather neglected and kind of invisible. After a while he got up to get a cup of coffee but couldn't find the break room. Finally, he flagged someone down in the hall and asked for directions. After returning to Patty's old desk, Bob just sat there and reflected. He didn't have access to a computer, didn't have an email address; in fact, he didn't even know how to get an outside line on the phone. All in all, it was pretty frustrating.

By lunchtime, there was still no Karen, so he decided to take the initiative and approach one of his new co-workers to go out to lunch with him. "Lunch?" his co-worker retorted. "Around here, lunch is a quick power bar or something out of the machine in the break room. We just don't take real lunches. You'll get used to it. We all did." Bob turned, made his way to the elevator and left the building for lunch.

When he returned, Karen was back in her office. "Bob, you're back! Sorry I wasn't here earlier. I got tied up in a meeting that

lasted longer than expected. I was disappointed you weren't here when I got back. No one seemed to know where you were."
"Oh, I just hopped out to grab a bite to eat for lunch," Bob replied. "Got it. Well, glad you kept yourself busy. We don't usually go out for lunch, but today's an exception, isn't it?! Janet said she parked you in Patty's old cube. I hadn't really worked out the details of where you'd be sitting, but that will do for now. Have you gotten your user access to the system yet?" "No," Bob responded. "I don't have a company email address either." "Well, don't worry. We'll have you set up in no time. I'll have the IT guys start working on it this afternoon."

"I need to put you to work right away, reviewing the results from last quarter's marketing campaigns. I have to present our findings at an executive meeting in the morning, so we'll have to work into the night. Hope you didn't have plans." As it turned out, Bob did have plans. He was supposed to take his wife and son out to dinner to celebrate his new job and then go to a movie. "No," Bob answered, I'm happy to stay and help." Disheartened, Bob returned to Patty's old desk, reflected on how to explain his day to his wife, and wondered what he had gotten himself into.

Of course, the way to avoid this dynamic is to establish each party's expectations right up front. Unlike romantic relationships, where there is a period of getting to know one another before making the decision to enter into a relationship, in an employment situation, that opportunity rarely exists. Therefore, it is essential for the manager, the team, and the organization to communicate their formal and informal expectations. And it is just as important that the individual communicate what they expect in return. It's a critical step in maximizing the likelihood that people stay engaged.

The expectations that need to be discussed and addressed make up a company's culture and the culture of a team. Therefore, it is essential that a leader be clear about how things really are when communicating their expectations, rather than how things ideally should be. A leader who espouses one set of values and behaviors but lives by a different set displays a lack of integrity.

The values and behaviors that need to be discussed and agreed upon are those that essentially define the personality of the organization. Most of them fall into three groups: 1) how we work, 2) how we act, and 3) how we interact.

How We Work

The values and behaviors pertaining to how work gets done are behaviors like style of working, time demands, autonomy, breaks, personal space, personal devices, quality of work, flexibility, work/ life balance, routine, well-being, purpose, service, and customer focus.

How We Act

The values and behaviors pertaining to how we act are values like integrity, honesty, pride, professionalism, personal responsibility, business ethics, trustworthiness, attitude, and being solution-oriented.

How We Interact

The values and behaviors pertaining to how we interact are values like respect, trust, appreciation, professionalism, having a constructive approach, being service-oriented, collaboration, inclusion, non-aggression, and sexual harassment.

Because much of how we act and interact at work is done habitually—without much thought—drawing our attention to each value and behavior helps us be aware of those values and behaviors, which in turn allows us to more effectively communicate them to new members of our team. You can find a useful checklist of values and behaviors to use as a memory jogger in the appendix at the back of this book.

What To Do

Don't assume people know what is expected of them, and clarify expectations. Don't assume or take for granted that everyone knows how things are at work. Hoping that each person will behave the way we want them to and that they will function with the same set of values we expect of our team will eventually lead to disappointment, conflict, and disillusionment. Communicate what you expect of each person and clarify what they expect in return. Sit down with each new person and help them understand the culture of your organization, the culture of your team, and the values you expect people to operate by. By eliminating surprises, you establish each party's expectations and ensure no one becomes disillusioned. When you help people understand what you expect and how they should function, you bring out the best in people.

Develop People

Develop people's thinking and judgment through coaching and mentoring.

Why It Matters

Very few people—if any—are at their full potential. People become stagnant in the absence of new challenges or when they're not pushed to stretch beyond their current abilities. Work becomes mundane and enthusiasm wanes in the face of routine. Additionally, without growth and development from the company and its leadership, people will begin to look elsewhere for new challenges. Lack of growth and lack of increased responsibility are leading causes of turnover within an organization. Therefore, if we want to bring out the best in people, we need to help them grow. It's an obligation that all leaders have. Plus, there is tremendous opportunity and satisfaction in developing people.

The first benefit, obviously, is to the person being developed. When we help someone expand their skill set and knowledge base, we make them more valuable and more versatile, which in turn instills a sense of pride. Instilling pride in work and workmanship is a cornerstone of the foundation for eliciting excellence. In addition, we demonstrate our belief in them, their abilities, and their potential, which nurtures loyalty and responsiveness.

The next way that developing people elicits excellence is the impact it has on our team. When individual members of a team grow their abilities and their value, they in turn inspire others to do the same. Even though you may not have personally worked with each member of your team (although hopefully you will at some point), the people you develop act as examples of what is possible, which, if you have the right people on your team, will act to motivate others to take the initiative to improve themselves for the betterment of their future and the benefit of the organization.

The third manner in which developing others brings forth excellence lies within us. By mastering the art of developing people, we become more skilled in our communication abilities, more effective in our leadership, and more leveraged in our efforts. All of these act to make us more productive, more creative, and more confident, thereby eliciting excellence within us.

Given the impact and far-reaching implications of developing others, it is critical to master this important competency. Professional growth occurs in two ways—by the acquisition of new skills and knowledge (hard skills), and by honing interpersonal and leadership competencies (soft skills). The acquisition of new skills and knowledge is relatively easy. They're effectively gained through training and reading. For example, one can easily become proficient in the use of new software by reading about it or attending a training workshop.

But when it comes to soft skills like interpersonal competencies, strategic thinking, judgment, and leadership effectiveness, it's a different story. People can't be trained in any of these competencies. Instead, they must be developed over time. The process of developing people consists of providing guidance through coaching and mentoring as opportunities present themselves, coupled with expansion of responsibility and authority. Adopting a coach-like approach with people is the fastest and most effective means of accomplishing this.

What does a coaching style of leadership look like? Being coach-like embodies a number of competencies and strategies that work in conjunction with one another. The most impactful behavior to master when it comes to coaching and mentoring is the act of asking rather than telling. Many of us, in an effort to help someone get it right (and in the name of expediency), tell others what to do and how to do it. And while this does get the work done, it does little to develop the other person, their skill set, or their confidence.

A coach-like approach would be to ask them what they would do and how they would do it instead of starting off by telling them what to do. This strategy serves a number of very important purposes. Firstly, it demonstrates that you have an interest in what they have to say. When you listen to what someone is telling you, it acts as a sign of respect. It demonstrates that you value their ideas. The next benefit of asking is that their answers will give you a sense of how they think. Their answers will reveal their level of insight and judgment and will illustrate their problem-solving abilities. And lastly, listening to the answers to your questions will provide clues as to how best to help them develop. It helps you understand which aspects of development they need help and guidance with.

Roger knocked on Susan's open door. He was stumped as to how to proceed with his plan but knew Susan would have the answer. "Hi, Roger. Come on in. What's up?" Susan asked, looking up from her work.

"I need your advice on something. I'm working on putting together that plan for updating that product we discussed, and I'm stuck," Roger replied. "OK, let me hear what you've got." Roger responded with the details of the plan he had developed so far. "My plan is to work with engineering to make some

modifications to the design and add some new features I've come up with. Once we have the redesign, I'll tell production what changes they need to make, and I'll offer training to the sales team to get them up to speed on the new features. I'm pretty clear about all that. The two things I'm stuck on are pricing and how to get it to market quickly."

Susan could quickly see a couple of mistakes Roger made in this thinking and planning, but instead of correcting him and sending him off in the right direction, she decided to ask him some questions.

"Sounds like you've given it a lot of thought, Roger," Susan responded. "Let me ask you a few questions. How did you come up with the new features you plan to add?" "Well," Roger replied, "I have been giving it a lot of thought and I decided these features would add the greatest value."

It had become evident that Roger had decided what was needed in the marketplace on his own, without getting any insights from the people who knew the customers' needs best: the sales team, the customer support department, and of course, the customers themselves. She could have explained why he should have talked to at least some of those people but instead chose to keep probing.

"Did you brainstorm with anyone else about them?" "No. But I'm pretty confident that I've nailed this." "Are there any other people who could offer insights into what customers want?" She wanted to see how good his judgment was once she began revealing his blind spot to him. After reflecting briefly, he responded, "Well, I guess I could check in with some of the sales guys to see *what they think." "I agree," Susan said. "They might pick up on something you missed."*

She continued to probe, still assessing his thinking, "Are there any other folks who might have ideas for what our customers want?" "Well, I suppose we could ask some of our customers directly." Susan agreed with him, replying, "Yes. I think we could. Would it also help to talk to the customer support folks?" Roger agreed it would.

"Let me ask you another question.... What other benefits could asking the sales team for their input have?" Roger paused for a minute as he shifted his thinking. "I think they'd be more enthusiastic about the new design." "Yes, " Susan said, continuing to mentor him. "Could involving them also help you price the new product?" "Yes! Absolutely!" Roger exclaimed as the light came on for him.

Susan continued, "And what are your thoughts about how to speed up the tooling and production to get it to market faster?" "I could bring the production people into the discussion with engineering right from the start," Roger replied. "Perfect!" Susan exclaimed. "Now you're on the right track." She had successfully begun to shift Roger's thinking and problem-solving skills. "Feeling better about getting your plan on track?" "You bet," he responded. "I'll let you know if I get stuck again."

"Fantastic," Susan replied. Just let me know if you need more help or hit a roadblock." Roger got up and headed back to his office, confident he had a sound approach for successfully bringing his plan to fruition.

An important strategy for bringing out the best in people is to coach and mentor them.

What To Do

Don't direct people and give them answers. Always giving people the answer keeps them from growing. While it's true that the work would get done faster if you gave answers right away, it doesn't generally improve their thinking or judgment. And while giving answers may be faster, it virtually ensures that they'll have to come back to you the next time the issue arises.

Ask good questions. Practice asking questions that give you insight into how a person thinks. Ask questions that reveal their judgment—ones that probe why they see things the way they do. Gaining these valuable insights will guide you as to how to best help and develop them.

Mentor people. Give people the benefit of your experience. Help them understand why and how you make your decisions. Share the mistakes you've made and the lessons you've learned.

Provide professional growth opportunities. Be on the lookout for development opportunities. Delegate meaningful tasks. Offer people training programs so they can learn new skills. Utilize executive coaches to provide outside perspective and objective input. Often, hearing guidance from someone else can have a greater impact and make all the difference.

Be Inspiring

Be someone people admire.

Why It Matters

Bringing out the best in people requires us to have the ability to inspire. In order for any of us to be our best, we need to be inspired. When we feel inspired, we aspire to accomplish more and reach new heights of success. Being inspired helps our resolve to overcome any fears, obstacles or challenges that may arise. And having inspiration sparks the imagination as to what is possible. It builds belief, enthusiasm and hope.

There's a difference between inspiration and motivation. The dictionary defines *inspire* as "To exert a stimulating or beneficial effect upon, or to arouse with a particular emotion." In contrast, *motivate* is defined as "To provide with an incentive or move to action."

Therefore, we inspire people by who *we* are and what *we* do or did, and we motivate people by who *they* are and what *they* want. In other words, inspiration is about us and motivation is about them.

When people are inspired by us, they tend to admire and respect us more. When we inspire people, they make an effort to emulate us and seek to earn our respect. A leader who inspires others and has their respect and admiration is better able to get people aligned with their passion, vision, or cause.

How does someone become inspiring? How does a person cause others to admire them? The clues can be found in studying the people who inspire us. Most everyone can think of people in their life or in public life (present or historic) who they find inspirational.

Some public figures who many people find inspiring are Theodore Roosevelt, Abraham Lincoln, Mahatma Gandhi, and Martin Luther King. Each of these people has inspired people to become more than they were.

How did they do that? What was it about them that acted as inspiration for so many? Here are the traits and actions that cause us to be inspired. It's not necessary to be or do all these things, but it is necessary that we embody some of them.

They effectively communicated and acted on a vision, passion, purpose, or philosophy that defined and motivated them. People are attracted to someone who stands for something. They admire and are inspired by someone who has conviction for and lives by a philosophy, purpose, or vision. Of course, to be a person who inspires others, we need to let people know what matters to us, and we need to act on that vision or passion. Actions speak louder than words.

They overcame adversity. People become inspired when they hear a story of someone who overcame adversity. When people hear a story of someone who overcame adversity and achieved success, it creates hope and a belief that they, too, can overcome their own obstacles and setbacks. A story of overcoming setbacks puts things in perspective for people and helps them realize that their situation isn't as bad as they originally thought. Here's an example of a great, inspiring, true story of someone who overcame adversity and achieved notable success.

This man worked his entire career and then retired. He received his first social security check and was dismayed at how small it was. He had worked his entire life and now he'd have to figure out how to live on such a small amount of money.

So he decided to do something about it. He took stock of all his assets, but in truth, he had none. In fact, the only thing he had that might be of any value—oddly enough—was a recipe. People loved his recipe, so he devised a plan. He took his recipe to the best restaurant in town and offered to give them his recipe. All he asked in return was for them to share any profits from the sales it generated. The restaurant said "No."

Not being discouraged, he took it to the next best restaurant in town. He made the same offer and, unfortunately, got the same answer. But he was determined to succeed. So he went to every restaurant in town. Everyone turned him down.

He started going to every restaurant in the county. No matter how much he modified his offer, each restaurant turned him away. Finally, he was going so far from his home, he couldn't get back at night. Here was this 65-year-old man, broke, sleeping in his car each night!

He was turned down over a 1,000 times in a row! And finally, on his 1,010th proposal, Harland Sanders got his "Yes". That's how Kentucky Fried Chicken got its start and how Harland Sanders became successful!

They stood up for what they believed in. Many people don't have the strength of their convictions. Talk is cheap, and someone who stands up for what they believe in or stands up for someone else they believe to be right is a person others admire. Someone who takes a stand inspires people—*whether or not they agree with them.*

They acted with and in integrity. When a leader has integrity and acts in a manner that reflects that integrity, they earn the admiration of others and inspire others by their actions.

Being an inspiring leader brings out the best in people.

What To Do

Don't use fear and intimidation to get results. Fear and intimidation simply get compliance. They don't bring out the best in people. Neither does using logic as a means of motivating people. People are motivated by who they are and what they want. They're not motivated by what you want. People decide to take action emotionally rather than by the logic of your argument. Help people feel what you feel and you'll help them aspire to be more than they currently are. You'll be a far more effective leader by inspiring others with your actions and your conviction to what matters to you.

Never miss the opportunity to share what matters to you. People are attracted to and respond to leaders who are passionate about something. When a leader is passionate, people will follow them and be inspired by them. Become clear on the values that matter most to you and let those around you know about them. Reflect throughout the day as to whether your actions are in alignment with those values you say matter. Leaders who live their values inspire people. (Conversely, saying one thing but doing another is not very inspiring.)

Share past challenges you've overcome. It doesn't have to be a major life-altering challenge; it can be any kind of physical, mental, or emotional challenge you overcame which made a difference in your life. People are inspired by those who overcame adversity.

Become a master storyteller. Use stories to make your point and paint a picture. People relate to stories and analogies, and when told effectively, they will evoke an emotional response. Stories can be very inspiring. Rather than simply relating the facts of a story, help the listener get a sense of how the person in the story (or you) felt in that moment. Putting the situation in some context will allow the listener to feel what was happening. Use descriptive words to paint the picture you'd like the listener to see in their mind's eye. Think of telling a story as an opportunity to be dramatic, using your voice and your speech pattern to give your story excitement, passion, frustration, joy, or any other appropriate emotion. The more people *feel* the events of a story, the better they can relate to it and the more you'll inspire them with it.

Be of Service

Ask how you can help.

Why It Matters

There's an interesting aspect to bringing out the best in people that's often overlooked. It's the matter of being of service as a leader. The most effective means of highlighting the importance of this attitude is by reflecting on the answers to a few questions.

The first question that needs to be asked is, "Who is the most important person to your company?" (Notice I didn't ask *in* your company, but rather *to* your company.) The answer, of course, is the customer. No customers = No company.

The next question to answer is, "Who is the most important person in your company to your customers?" Clearly the answer is not "the CEO." In fact, customers generally don't interact with *any* of the executives within a company. No, the most important person to a customer is the person they come in contact with: the front-line people. These are usually sales and customer service/support professionals.

The final question is the one that really drives this leadership point home. "What then is the job of the manager of those front-line people?" The job of that manager is to ensure that each person is able to do their work as effectively, as professionally, and as enjoyably as possible. People want to do a good job. They want to make customers happy and ensure they are satisfied. They want to make sure they enhance the image, brand, and reputation of the company. And they want to be viewed by customers, peers, and others in the organization as professionals.

If people don't have the right tools, knowledge, and environment to perform at their best, then frustration and disillusionment set in. It begins to feel like the leadership and the organization don't really care about them. It begins to feel like their work is somehow unimportant. And by saying one thing (how important their role is) but doing another (not taking action to improve the environment), it demonstrates a lack of integrity on the part of the leaders.

The dynamic that occurs isn't simply about increasing productivity. When a leader is mindful of the needs of his or her team and demonstrates that he or she is looking out for their well-being, it builds trust and respect, leading to higher engagement, greater loyalty, and better response to initiatives.

What exactly does a leader have to do to demonstrate they value their team and to be of service? The manager must ensure that his team has the training and knowledge they need. She needs to provide the support and the environment to allow them to be their best. And the leader needs to make sure they have the tools and information they need to do their best work. The whole goal is to make their work as enjoyable, productive, and rewarding as possible. If this leadership philosophy permeates the entire organization, the organizational chart begins to look like an inverted pyramid instead of the traditional top-down pyramid structure.

This isn't simply a theory or a type of feel-good culture that compromises profit and performance. Far from it. It is a practical, proven, and extremely effective approach to conducting business. Here are three examples of businesses that have embraced a servant leader philosophy and have not only done well but have out-paced their competitors by orders of magnitude.

The first example is a relatively small, privately held company in Denver. It's in an industry where many of their competitors are struggling just to survive. However, this company made a seven-figure profit! The owner adopted a philosophy of helping those around him to become successful. He applied this philosophy to his employees, his customers, and even his vendors. After interviewing the owner and his employees, it became apparent that his team was loyal, enthusiastic, professional, free from stress, and highly productive. The results of service-minded leadership speak for themselves.

The second example is Frontier Airlines. In an industry plagued by stagnant growth and evaporating profits, this company adopted a servant leader approach to business and out-paced its competition by leaps and bounds—both in growth and profits. By way of example, when the office closes for a holiday, many of the office staff will go into the field to help the front-line folks with the heavy holiday workload. Servant leaders abound within the organization.

The third example is Nucor Steel, which ended up dominating the U.S. steel industry by adopting a servant leader, almost egalitarian, business model. The leadership of the company minimized the perceived differences between the front line and the management/executive team. It became a company that recognized the important role each person plays in the success of the organization.

Being of service to the people you lead helps bring out the best in them.

What To Do

Don't ignore or pay lip service to your team. By not addressing the practical needs of the people who work for you, you hamper their productivity and creativity, create undue stress and frustration, and demonstrate you don't care about them. If you talk about helping but don't actually do anything, it demonstrates a lack of integrity—and trust and respect are diminished.

Ask how you can help. Find out what you can do to make their job easier, more productive, and more enjoyable. Ensure they have the right tools and information for the work they do. Make sure they have the proper skills and knowledge to perform efficiently and effectively. And do your best to establish a physical and cultural environment that helps them feel good about coming to work.

Stand up for your people. Don't simply go through the motions of asking for the improvements that have been asked for. Fight for the needs of your team in order to make a real difference. It demonstrates loyalty to and concern for the people you lead. Truly be of service.

Lead Appropriately

Be the leader people need in the moment.

Why It Matters

Some leaders lead with a very inclusive, collaborative style, while others are more of the command and control ilk. Some like to foster a fast-paced environment, while others favor a culture of autonomy. And they are all effective. Sometimes.

The underlying problem is that in order to bring out the best in people, different situations call for different styles of leadership. If the situation calls for a strong hand and a leader spends lots of time trying to build consensus, events may overtake the process, making it moot and undermining the success of a company. Conversely, if the situation cries out for alignment and buy in but the leader dictates to his or her team and demands action, the results will generally be mediocre and the team left disillusioned.

An effective leader understands that different situations call for different styles of leading and knows when and how to use each style. There are three general approaches to leadership, and each is useful in the right situation. The first is a commanding style of leadership. The second style of leading is one of inspiration and vision. And the third is a style that focuses on building consensus and buy in.

When an organization falls into times of crisis, uncertainty abounds. Fears about the future proliferate, and hard decisions must be made. The problem is that because no one can accurately see into the future, the most effective course of action is unclear. Often, a sense of urgency exists, adding to the anxiety and stress within the organization.

In cases such as this, a leader can't afford to rely too heavily on those around him or her. He or she simply doesn't have the luxury of taking the time to build consensus or wait for elaborate plans to be developed by others. The very nature of the crisis requires a leader to step up, take control, make decisions, and command that certain actions be taken. In order for people to be their best in times of crisis, a leader must alleviate fears about the future and provide a sense of security. In times like this, a command and control style of leadership is most appropriate.

The truth is, however, that most companies are *not* in crisis mode. In the absence of crisis, a command-control style of leadership is rarely effective.

The next style of leadership is characterized by vision and inspiration. When an organization finds itself in a period of stagnation or contraction, the future becomes uncertain. Some people within the organization begin to flounder, struggling to keep things moving forward. They may resign themselves to treading water, hoping to ride out a slump. Others may decide to work harder (and harder still), looking to overcome the lackluster performance. And yet others may decide that new ideas are called for. These are typically modifications to existing products, services or processes. Sometimes the ideas are good, but of course, many times they are ideas born out of desperation and, as such, they make little sense. While some of these ideas may have value and create better results, generally, the improvement in results is modest.

In times like this, what's called for is a leader with vision—a leader who can paint a picture of a very different future and inspire the organization. It requires that a leader have a clear, well-defined picture of a new direction. The organization needs a leader who can light a fire within the organization and spark people into action with hope, creativity, pride, and enthusiasm.

But for most companies, neither crisis nor the need for a new vision exists. Most companies are in the mode of driving growth and profitability in their existing business model. For these companies, a leader needs to foster collaboration and alignment. It's the best way to improve engagement. Bringing people together enhances buy in and removes roadblocks. A leader who can bring everyone together and get them pulling in the same direction will produce superior results.

If a leader uses a controlling approach in this situation, he or she will undermine the potential available from their team. If a leader focuses on a new vision, or worse, a flavor-of-the-month approach—jumping from one initiative to another—he or she confuses the team, ruins productivity, creates frustration, and kills momentum.

Using the right leadership style for a given situation is essential for bringing out the best in people.

What To Do

Don't be one dimensional. Just as we tend to communicate in our primary social style, we also tend to lead in the style we're most comfortable with and used to. Leading the same way all the time can sabotage the productivity and success of an organization.

Be the person people need in the moment. Learn to use the appropriate style when the situation calls for something different. Have a strong hand when people need someone to take charge. Take a step back from the day-to-day events when a new vision and direction are called for. And build consensus when the company needs energizing and more enthusiasm.

CHAPTER 6: BLUEPRINT FOR SUCCESS

How and Where to Begin

We've discussed the many ways to bring out the best in people. Each of the competencies is important and effective, and while most of us are naturally good at a number of them, most leaders acknowledge that there is always room for improvement.

The challenge is that with the demands our existing workload places on our time and effort, it's impractical to work on improving them all at the same time. We simply don't have that luxury.

Not only that, but the truth is that it's difficult, if not impossible, to truly determine which competencies would have the greatest impact on our leadership effectiveness. After all, it's not how well *we* think we're doing that matters. It's how well those around us think we're doing.

Here are the four steps necessary to become a highly effective leader and bring out the best in people:

- **Step One: Conduct an Initial Survey**
- **Step Two: Conduct an In-Depth Assessment**
- **Step Three: Conduct 360° Leadership Assessments**
- **Step Four: Address the Issues.**

Step One: Conduct an Initial Survey

Determine the Need

The first step is to get a general sense of how well the organization as a whole is bringing out the best in people. Conduct a simple survey to determine just how engaged and fulfilled the people in your organization are. There are certain telltale signs that indicate whether people are engaged, ambivalent about their work, or generally unhappy with the way things are.

Ask if they feel good about the work they do and whether they get absorbed in their work. Ask if they lose track of time when they work (a great indicator that their work matters to them). Ask if they look forward to coming to work and enjoy it. Ask them (anonymously) whether they feel they give their best effort. Find out if they think about finding better ways to do things and whether they think about work outside of normal business hours. The answers to these questions and others will reveal how enthused a person is about working at your organization.

With these insights, you'll be able to determine the levels of engagement with the organization. There are four levels of workforce engagement: highly engaged, engaged, ambivalent, and actively disengaged. Obviously it's not realistic for everyone to be highly engaged all the time, but clearly, you'll want the highly engaged and engaged groups to be as large as possible and the actively disengaged group to be as small as possible.

My firm uses our *"Professional Fulfillment Survey"* to determine overall levels of engagement. You can download a sample of this survey from our website here:

http://www.elicitingexcellence.com/pfs

Use the code **EEPFS** to access it.

Step Two: Conduct an In-Depth Assessment

Identify the Issues within the Organization

If your results aren't what you'd like them to be, you'll need to ascertain specifically which issues are undermining our attempts to elicit excellence. The areas to examine fall into the major categories of Maslow's Hierarchy of Needs—physiology, security, belonging, self-esteem, and self-fulfillment. Conduct an in-depth assessment to reveal the areas that should be addressed.

The assessment should ascertain whether people feel they're being fairly compensated, along with whether they feel their health and well-being are being provided for. This includes the health and well-being of their families. Next, the assessment should determine whether people generally have positive expectations with respect to the company's future, along with their expectations regarding their future with the company. Your assessment should ascertain whether people feel there is good communication from senior leadership and if there is a sense of cohesiveness within the organization, especially on the team level. Assess whether people feel they're valued and respected by the organization and by their leaders. Value and respect are reflected in the work they're tasked with and how much freedom they're given in the execution of that work. Assess all the areas around trust, respect, and value. The final area that needs to be assessed pertains to personal growth. Determine whether people feel they are getting the opportunity to grow professionally.

My firm uses our "*Company Personality Assessment*" to determine the specific areas that are causing disillusionment and disengagement. You can download a sample of this assessment from our website here:

http://www.elicitingexcellence.com/cpa

Use the code **EECPA** to access it.

Step Three: Conduct 360° Leadership Assessments

Identify the Issues within the Leaders

Most executives feel they are good leaders. Even though leaders will acknowledge that there is room for improvement, none feels he or she is poor. Yet, we all know (or have known) some pretty poor leaders. The truth is that it's difficult for us to determine whether we're good at leading; it's challenging for several reasons.

1) The first challenge is that quality of leadership is determined by those being led, rather than by the leader. How we view ourselves is fairly irrelevant. Even when we feel we have a good read on how others regard us, we're frequently too lenient or too hard on ourselves. We tend to overestimate our effectiveness or are overly self-critical. It's very difficult to determine how others really view us until we get objective feedback. What matters more is how we're viewed by others, and only they can tell us whether we're effective.

2) The second challenge is that we all have blind spots. No matter how experienced we are, how intelligent we are, or how much education we've had, each of us has blind spots, and no amount of thinking can reveal them. Almost always, it takes someone else to point them out to us.

3) The third issue is that rarely is a leader excellent in all competencies, and just as rare are leaders who are devoid of all the essential competencies. The truth is that leadership competencies are on a continuum. Leadership competencies are a matter of degree and quality.

The only way for a leader to objectively evaluate the competencies that need to be addressed is by conducting a 360° leadership assessment. A properly designed assessment will solicit anonymous feedback from all those who interact with the leader on a variety of meaningful competencies. Since the need for confidentiality and anonymity is so great, online assessments are ideal. In addition to the rating of a leader's competencies, a well-designed assessment will also provide for anonymous written feedback—especially as it pertains to the competencies which receive a low score.

The assessment should include all the competencies addressed in Chapter 3. My firm uses an online 360° assessment that does just that. A list of the competencies is available for download from our website here:

http://www.elicitingexcellence.com/leadership

Use the code **EE360** to access it.

Step Four: Address the Issues

Address the issues with each leader

Once the issues causing people to disengage and do less than their best have been determined, those issues need to be addressed, disengagement needs to be reversed, and an environment must be created to help people re-engage.

Create leadership development plans for each key leader based on the results of his or her 360 assessment. Despite the hundreds of books, programs, and websites devoted to leadership, the truth is that leaders can't be trained. Leaders need to be developed. Hopefully this doesn't seem like a simple matter of semantics, because it isn't.

Leadership is more about who you are than about what you do or what you know. Two executives can do and say the same things but get very different results—even when they do and say those things to the very same people! Although what you say and what you do are important, effective leadership is even more dependent upon how you do or say those things. This explains why the actions of those two executives can elicit such different responses. People respond to us based on who we are, and it's this *how* of doing, saying, and being that defines who we are seen to be.

You can train people about what to say. You can train people about what to do. You can even show someone how to do and say those things. But getting them to change how they go about doing things and getting them to change how they go about saying things is a whole other story. Many aspects of how we interact, react, and respond are done out of habit and, as such, are difficult to change on our own. In fact, we're often blind to our habits, since by definition, we act out our habits without giving them much thought.

The bottom line is that in order for someone to hone weaker leadership competencies and break old habits, it usually requires outside perspective from a trusted source. (It's one of the main reasons that executive coaching has become so popular and is so effective.)

Summary

The most efficient and effective means of improving how well we bring out the best in people is to assess the areas causing disengagement, determine which leaders could be more effective, and then assess which competencies each leader is good at along with which ones should be bolstered. Once the areas of focus are determined, put a plan of development into action. This affords the quickest and most impactful means of bringing out the best in people.

If you'd like help in assessing and developing these competencies in yourself or your leaders, please contact us. We specialize in helping leaders bring out the best in people.